Gender or Giftedness

A challenge to rethink the basis for leadership within the Christian community

A study on the role of women

Second edition

Lynn Smith

Gender or Giftedness was originally printed in Manila, The Philippines, for the World Evangelical Fellowship Commission on Women's Concerns, March 2000

Reprinted May 2009.

Scripture quotations taken from the

HOLY BIBLE, NEW INTERNATIONAL VERSION.

Copyright 1973, 1978, 1984 by International Bible Society.

Used by permission of Zondervan Publishing House. All rights reserved.

National Library of Canada Cataloguing in Publication

Smith, Lynn

Gender or Giftedness/ Lynn Smith

ISBN 978-0-9810460-0-6

Copyright © 2000, 2009 Lynn Smith

To order: Search online or contact Lynn Smith lynn@smithhouse.ca

Dedicated to the women in my life:

- my mother, Mary Frances, who inspired me by leading the way with courage and humour in an age that restricted women;

- my daughter, Julie, and daughter-in-law, Miriam, whose example encourages me to live more fully in the freedom and opportunity that God has given me;

- my granddaughters, Alicia, Lindsay, and Jacqueline, whose young lives challenge me to work to create for them a culture that does not diminish or restrict them in any way because they are female.

I am blessed to have this community of female companions - and doubly blessed to have the encouragement of the men in my family: father, husband, sons, son-in-law and grandsons. My prayer is that individually and together we may respond to the call of God upon our lives.

Contents

PREFACE to the First Edition	vii
PREFACE to the Second Edition	iix
PROLOGUE	x

CHAPTER 1 INTRODUCING THE STUDY

A. Reason for the Study	1
B. Goal of the Study	2
C. Interpretative Principles for the Study	5
Discussion and Reflection Questions	6

CHAPTER 2 INVESTIGATING PARADIGMS

A. Seeking a Biblical Paradigm	7
B. Examining the Traditional Paradigm	11
C. Accepting Jesus' Paradigm	13
Discussion and Reflection Questions	15

CHAPTER 3 INTERPRETING SCRIPTURE

A. The Old Testament	17
1. Creation	17
2. Expanded Story of Creation	19
3. Relationship Spoiled by Sin	23
4. The Female in the Old Testament	27
5. Prophecy of a New Paradigm	34

Discussion and Reflection Questions	36
B. The New Paradigm of Redemption	38
1. The Cultural Setting	38
2. The Attitude Required	39
3. The Teaching and Modeling of Jesus	40
4. The Fulfillment of Joel's Prophecy	49
5. The Teaching of Paul	50
6. The Church's Demonstration of the New Model	82
Discussion and Reflection Questions	85

CHAPTER 4 IDENTIFYING CULTURAL INFLUENCES

A. Acknowledging Personal Beliefs	87
B. Shaping of Beliefs	88
1. View of Women in Judaism	88
2. View of Women in the Early Church	88
3. View of Women in the First Few Centuries	89
4. View of Women in the Middle Ages	92
5. View of Women in the Modern Period	92
6. Role of Women Today	93
C. Challenging Biases	96
Discussion and Reflection Questions	98

CHAPTER 5 IMPLEMENTING A RESPONSE

A. Develop a Vision	103

B. Define Beliefs Related to that Vision	104
1. Beliefs Related to Controversial Definitions	105
2. Beliefs Related to Biblical Authority	106
3. Beliefs Related to Community	107
4. Beliefs Related to Feminism	109
5. Beliefs Related to Giftedness	110
6. Beliefs Related to Leadership	111
7. Beliefs Related to Interpretive Principles	112
8. Beliefs Related to Cultural Restrictions	112
C. Discern the Present Reality	114
D. Design Goals to Move from Reality to Vision	114
E. Determine the Available Resources	115
F. Decide on the Action	115
G. Do it...Then Evaluate and Revise Goals.	116
Discussion and Reflection Questions	117
EPILOGUE	118
ENDNOTES	125
BIBLIOGRAPHY	136
APPENDIX A Glossary of Definitions	141
APPENDIX B Two Different Paradigms	146
ABOUT THE AUTHOR	149

PREFACE to the First Edition

The desire to have study material available on the role of Christian women in the home, church and society was clearly articulated at the conference of the World Evangelical Fellowship Commission on Women's Concerns in Manila in 1992. As the representatives from around the world presented the needs of women in their own countries, it became evident that while the severity of the needs varied, they were basically the same three: the need for *education*, the need for *encouragement* and the need for *example* - meaning role models and/or mentoring.

When the area of education was discussed, it became clear that the needs ranged from basic literacy in some parts of the world, to the need for advanced training in management and leadership skills in other parts of the world. It also became clear that for many women, regardless of the part of the world in which they lived, the traditional teaching of the church that women are to be under the authority of men and thus subservient to men presents an insurmountable barrier for women to appropriate the education that is available in their culture. Christian women who CAN avail themselves of the opportunity for education may not be able to use their learning within the church setting. When men hold the position of authority, whether the issue is illiteracy or lack of managerial training, the freedom of women to benefit from education is restricted by what men will permit.

It seemed wise, then, to undergird whatever other educational programs were developed, with study material that would help both men and women rethink the traditional teaching on the role of women. In order for Christian women to move out of the cycle of poverty and exploitation, they need to know that their efforts are consistent with the truth of Scripture. In order for women to use their gifts in response to the call of God, and in order for Christian men to encourage women into new areas of service, they must know that they are being true to Scripture.

This study material was developed to respond to the need for education in this area. The functioning of women within the community of faith is addressed from the perspective of spiritual gifting, by asking the questions, "Does gender determine ministry or does ministry flow out of call and giftedness?" and "On what basis do we make this decision?"

It is offered to churches in honour of their women who long to serve God with enthusiasm, dedication, passion and with all of their gifts. May it serve to bring new hope and new vitality to the church of Jesus Christ - around the world.

PREFACE to the Second Edition

Since the original printing in 2000, *Gender or Giftedness* has been translated into Arabic, Croatian, French and German and, as well, a culturally adapted English version has been published in India. The messages that have come as a result have clearly indicated that there was a need for a book that surveyed and condensed the current literature for the average reader. There are many books which give a more in-depth theological or cultural treatment of the topic. My intention was to write for the men and women in the pew or the pulpit who do not have the time to research for themselves but who sincerely want a biblical understanding of the role of women in the kingdom. I wanted to shift us from arguing about the difficult texts to creating a framework within which to understand those texts.

To the degree that I have been successful in doing that, I am content.

It was not my intention to reprint but just as I distributed my final copies, I began to get requests for more and I realized that the need was still there.

The changes have been minimal; however, I have updated the Bibliography in order to include some excellent books which have either been written, or that I have found, since publishing the first edition.

My desired outcome for the book has not changed. I believe that God wants both men and women to fulfill their calling as godly image bearers in the world – using their gifts to build up one another for the furthering of God's Kingdom. I offer it again with the prayer that it will stimulate healthy discussion about the role of women in the church.

PROLOGUE

The Bible calls us to a vision - a vision of life in the Kingdom of God. What does that look like to you? There are no doubt many images that would suffice - although none of them adequately - to help us visualize what life would look like lived in the realm where Christ reigns. Scripture gives us the image of a body working together to build itself up - each part doing its share according to the function intended for it. Scripture also talks about us being a people - a holy nation - a community of believers who worship, learn, and serve together. The question that will be asked of you in this study - and to which you will need to give an answer - is, "What are the requirements for service and leadership within this community?"

Certainly, the first requirement for service and leadership within this community is to be a member of the community and the basis for membership is redemption by the blood of Christ. This study will present redemption as the paradigm or framework which ought to govern our interpretation of the passages of Scripture which determine the basis for service and leadership within the church. In doing so, the hope is that the study will communicate a vision of the community Christ longs for us to enjoy - and provide you with some tools for moving that vision into reality.

My desire is that, as a result of this study, both men and women will be freed to respond to the call of God upon their lives, to build their community into a vibrant, living body of Christ and to then work together in unity, as one body, to challenge the societal values that victimize or keep in bondage (whether by race, class or gender) those whom Christ has set free.

I trust that both men and women will be challenged to move out in the power of the Spirit to do whatever God calls them to in their culture in the name of Christ.

Chapter 1
INTRODUCING THE STUDY

*The challenge here
is to accept the need
to rethink our views*

A. Reason for the Study

The challenge to rethink the traditional interpretation of the Biblical message as it pertains to women - and specifically their leadership role within the church - comes from the serious and honest questions which are being asked of the church.

Some of the questions arise from the media focus on the current global situation for both women and children. Why has the church allowed abuse and exploitation to continue, even within its own numbers, silencing the voice of those who try to speak up in order to alleviate their situation?

Some questions arise because the role of women in almost every culture is changing. Change is always unsettling and responses vary. Some embrace the changes without question, leaving those around them bewildered; others resist and struggle, but the result for everyone is confusion. Christian women are struggling with the conflict between what they believe God has gifted and called them to do and what churches will allow them to do. What should the response of the church be to these changes in the culture?

Other questions are raised because the scholarship of both men and women is revealing both biases and outright inaccuracies in Biblical translations which have formed our understanding of what the Bible

> *Rebecca Merrill Groothius[1] in Good News for Women points out that early church fathers accepted that Junia, who along with Andronicus is praised by Paul as "outstanding among the apostles" was both a woman and an apostle. However, more recent scholars "have earnestly endeavoured to explain that Junia was either not a woman, or if a woman, not an apostle but merely esteemed by the apostles".*
>
> *This they did on the basis of their prior belief that an apostle had to be male. And then, in order to make the text fit their assumptions, translators have in some cases changed her name to Junias (NIV).*

teaches about the role of women (see side bar). How do churches deal with the varying and often contradictory interpretations of the many passages of Scripture which speak of women?

Still other questions come from the study of church history which reveals how the church throughout its existence has changed its views of the value of women (see Chapter 4).

Women are wanting - and needing - to know if they can respond to the call of God on their lives and still be consistent with the teachings of Scripture. They need to know how they can maintain the integrity of Scripture and still use their gifts for the building up of others within their community of faith.

This struggle is creating a need to clarify what Scripture is really saying about the role of women and to determine the basis for making decisions about leadership in the church.

B. Goal of the Study

The goal of this study material is to help churches develop a working framework (paradigm) to address the issue of where women fit in their community while maintaining both unity and Biblical integrity.

Most Christians are serious about wanting to obey the Word of God and so come to the discussion about the appropriate functions for women in the church with a genuine desire to find the will of God. Most of us, however, are unaware that, along with that desire, we bring two things which may interfere with the discovery of God's truth.

The first is an interpretive framework - a window through which we view and therefore understand the Biblical message. Often this framework is not a consciously chosen one, but it is there nonetheless. It could be that we view all of Scripture through the window of Creation, or the Fall, or Redemption, or Heaven, or personal experience, or economics; but, whatever it is, until it is examined, we will not be aware of how it influences how we see and therefore interpret the biblical message.

In our attempt to determine what Scripture says about women, we usually begin immediately to look at the various Scripture passages that are relevant. Two dangers exist: one is that the Scripture that is chosen as relevant depends on our already established position; and the other is that Scripture appears to say what we already believe it says. It is difficult to come with eyes that are not clouded by preconceived ideas in order to see new things, or at least to not have our current perspective simply reinforced.

We need to be conscious of the fact that the framework **through which** we see a text will determine what we see **in** the text. The questions we bring **to** the text will determine what we get **out** of the text. The wrong window can blind us to the truth. The church has often had to rethink, in light of new evidence, what it was teaching as God's truth. The issue of slavery is one obvious illustration that the church has not always been right. W. Ward Gasque, in an article, "The Role of Women in the Church, in Society and in the Home," remarks that:

> until the middle of the nineteenth century most Christians believed that slavery was a divine institution because Paul says very emphatically that slaves are to obey their masters! A few verses from Paul and Peter were used as proof-texts to oppose a small band of forward looking Christians and others of their day who felt that the whole idea of slavery was an affront to the dignity and worth of man as made in the image of God.[2]

By seeing Scripture through the window of economics, many Christians were able to find support for their practice of slavery, even claiming that it was ordained by God.

Tradition is the second thing that may interfere with the discovery of God's truth. Traditional culture is a powerful influence and it varies from place to place and from time to time. When the traditional culture of the church comes up against the traditional culture of the surrounding society, there is bound to be conflict. When this happens, the church often retrenches, retreats and reinforces its position instead of allowing the culture to challenge its practices.

A good example of how the church refused, in spite of scientific evidence, to question its established teaching was when it excommunicated Galileo for teaching that the world was round and not flat as they had traditionally believed. It took the church 350 years to admit its error and forgive him. There are times when the church needs to be challenged to rethink its theology and its traditional perspective. A challenge can be an opportunity to discover truth.

When the role of women in the church is seen simply as a cultural issue, the argument can be made that any change of practice permitted by the church is allowing culture to determine its theology. If, however, the role of women is recognized as a theological issue which culture is forcing the church to reexamine, then truth can win out over tradition.

The goal of this study, then, is to identify an appropriate window for interpreting Scripture in order to move the discussion away from traditional practice and focus on the biblical basis for service within the body of Christ. For that reason, specific issues such as: controversial definitions of words (e.g. head covering, silence, or authority); the balance of power between men and women; and hierarchy versus equality, need to be set aside until a clear biblical framework for examination is established.

Then, when the framework is established, principles can be clarified and applied wherever the church is found. When a vision or principle is clear, the work of each person and each church is to ask, "How, in our particular culture, do we move toward that principle and what are the specific issues we need to address and specific steps we need to take?"

C. Interpretative Principles for the Study

Before beginning to look for a framework or window through which to interpret the passages regarding women, it is important to clarify the basic interpretive principles upon which this study is based[3]. The following premises have formed the basis for interpretation:

1. Respect for Scripture means that no text can be simply discarded as meaningless.

2. Scripture does not contradict itself. Where contradictions seem to emerge, it is not Scripture which is at fault, but our understanding of what the author intended the text to convey.

3. The context and the specific situation being addressed needs to be considered to determine why Paul says different things at different times.

4. Paul does not say one thing and do another. Congruency can be found between his words and his actions.

5. Jesus came to break both the power and the patterns of sin in the world.

6. The early church began to live out the good news of the gospel in an appropriate way.

7. We are called to investigate the principles of Scripture and discern their relevance to our own culture.

8. The message of the gospel remains consistent, even though its emphasis may change according to the needs of the culture it addresses.

Discussion and Reflection Questions

1. Why have you chosen to begin this study? What issues or questions do you bring to the discussion?

   If you are doing this study on your own, write down your issues and/or questions and keep them for later review. If you are in a group, be sure your issues are heard by the group. Later you will want to return to them.

2. What is your current vision for how men and women ought to minister together in the church, home and society?

3. How would you reconcile the call of God with the restrictions of the church?

4. What is your understanding of the criteria for service within the body of Christ?

5. Describe what an ideal community looks like to you.

6. What inconsistencies do you see, if any, in the teaching regarding women?

7. How would you answer those who, in their efforts to gain equality for women, choose to abandon Scripture because they see it as patriarchal and therefore not relevant for today?

Chapter 2
INVESTIGATING PARADIGMS

The challenge here is to assess the paradigms which govern interpretations

A. Seeking a Biblical Paradigm

Any challenge to the Biblical truth **must** be taken seriously and serious answers given. There are those who would entrench themselves in the "traditional" teaching without giving serious thought to the inconsistencies they both live and teach.

Others would use the framework of experience to interpret Scripture and come to the conclusion that the experience of women requires us to abandon Scripture because it is patriarchal and cannot be relevant for today.

Neither position deals with Scripture with adequate integrity. Instead, we must approach the texts with eyes to see and ears to hear God's message for the church today. We need to look for clear biblical teaching that seeks to find God's principles rather than either retreating into unexamined tradition or throwing out Scripture as irrelevant.

Those of us who want to wrestle adequately with Scripture must:

- allow culture to challenge our views but not determine them
- allow tradition to inform us but not confine us.

The place to begin is with an understanding of the overriding message of Scripture and to choose a framework that is consistent with that message.

From Genesis through Revelation, the predominant theme is that God created, and continuously calls into a personal relationship with Himself and with one another, those who will worship Him in Spirit and in truth; those who will love their God and one another. See Figure 1 (next page) for a diagram of God's interaction with His people.

Genesis 1 and 2 describe Creation:

> God created both a unity and a community when he created humanity as male and female: differentiated, yet united. Their diversity is clear: they are created male and female. But their unity is also clear: one flesh becoming two creatures.[1] And it is because of their unity that they enjoy companionship and community. It is their unity, their "one flesh" both prior to and following the creative act, that rules out hierarchy in Genesis 1 and 2.[2]

Genesis 3 tells about the Fall which ushered in the reign of sin:

> When sin entered, the first thing to go was oneness. Adam and Eve hid from God and from each other, they refused responsibility for their actions, and one became ruler, the other subject. It was a distortion of community.[3] The equality of their union was lost.

The remaining chapters of the Old Testament portray the story of God's interaction with His rebellious people and the establishing of various covenants with his people which tend to be grouped together by Christians into what is termed the "Old Covenant."

> Babel was a further distortion of community. In time, Abraham was to be the father of one family (community) but that community ended up in slavery.

> Then God called Moses to lead them out - to make them into a nation, a community whose God was Yahweh, a kingdom of priests accountable to God and servants of one another. God provided them with Judges to call them back to himself but they wanted Kings. They ended up with a divided kingdom and they fell. The community was gone once again.[4]

But God continued to call his people back into a relationship with Himself. The prophecies spoke of something new that God would do for his people, and the prophecy of Joel affirmed that when the Spirit was poured out women would be included in a new way.

In the New Testament, Christ enters the scene bringing REDEMPTION and the new covenant:

> He established a new community, a royal priesthood, his body. He was the life giver. Through his death, this community was given birth. But before he died, He modeled the kind of mature community we are expected to live. He prayed for oneness. He talked about one flock, one body.[5]

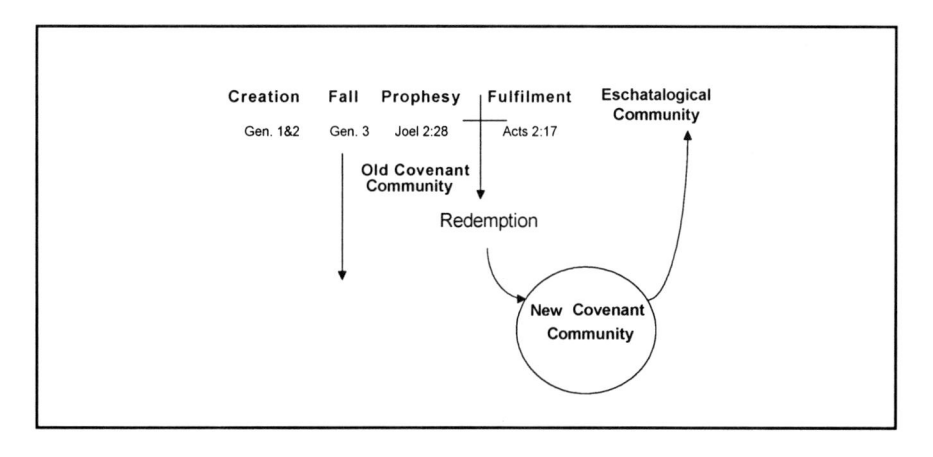

Figure 1

Clearly, God expects us to work at creating this kind of community here and now. The New Testament Scriptures show us the way

Christians, aided by the Holy Spirit, are to mature in beliefs, attitudes and relationships in the present, reflecting more and more accurately the eternal community we will enjoy when Christ returns.

Men and women were created to be in relationship with God and with one another; chosen to be a holy nation, a royal priesthood; redeemed to be the body of Christ; expected to live here on earth in community, in harmony and unity, with Christ as the head; commanded to submit to one another in love within this community of faith and by doing so to reveal the true nature of God to the world around us; and eventually to join the hosts of heaven in eternal worship and praise of our God. As Stan Grenz and Denise Muir Kjesbo state in *Women in the Church*, the "community of faith [is to] proclaim the gospel and live in the world as the company of those who acknowledge in the present the coming reign of God."[6]

Christ is the person to whom all of the Old Testament points, and from whom all the New Testament flows. His redemption is the action which is foreshadowed in the old covenant and fulfilled in the new covenant. Only the redeemed are the people of God; only the redeemed are the body of Christ; only the redeemed fulfill their destiny of being in relationship with God; only the redeemed are the holy nation, a royal priesthood; only the redeemed can reveal the true nature of God; only the redeemed have life "in Christ" for eternity. Because we have been created and redeemed for eternity, the new life we live here on earth is to be lived in a way that foreshadows the life to come.

It is redemption which reveals the whole plan of God, which permits us to keep the big picture in mind as we interpret Scripture, and which therefore becomes the logical framework through which to understand all of Scripture. When we look specifically at the role of women in the church, however, it is easy to interpret specific passages using another framework - using an incomplete view without even realizing it because of how we have been taught. Throughout the study, we will be looking for consistency, and it will become clear how differing frameworks can result in different interpretations.

B. Examining the Traditional Paradigm

Most Christians who have grown up in the church have been taught a patriarchal, hierarchical model for relationships between men and women, and thus also for the role of women within the church. Within this traditional model, the function of women is restricted by gender, whereas men are encouraged to function according to abilities, gifts and call. Patriarchy, the social order into which Christ came, is perceived by traditionalists to be the determinant form for Christianity for all time.

Also, since one of the consequences of sin was that Adam would rule over Eve, it is perceived that this aftermath of judgment is to determine the norm for men and women for all time. When the framework of the fall is the one through which Scripture is interpreted, the reign of sin becomes prescriptive (suggesting that God prescribes or determines that we must continue to suffer the effects of sin) rather than descriptive (which suggests that God is describing what the consequences of sin will be). The natural outcome is to see the effects of sin as established by God.

Faith Martin points out that so much of what molds our lives does not come from written laws but from a tradition - codes of civilization so powerful, so elementary, that we do not question their validity. She challenges us to move out from that cultural bondage. As an illustration of the fact that we ought to question the code that has placed women in subjection; that, in fact, an entire civilization can be wrong, Martin details the situations in cultures where female circumcision is practised, where because of poverty a destitute mother who needs a son in order to ensure her own survival is likely to wean a daughter from the breast as early as possible in order to enhance her chances of becoming pregnant again, and where the dowry system means that "sons bring wealth to the family, but daughters take it away."[7]

One of the main characteristics of this traditional view is that authority is given to men but not to women. As a result, authority is often seen to reside in the male leader rather than in the word of God or in the community, and submission is taught as submission of the woman (or wife) to the man (or husband).

Since power is understood as residing in a man who is in authority, any effort on the part of women to gain equality is seen as usurping the rightful power of men and, therefore, as a move against the will of God and is to be resisted.

This results either in the acceptance of the traditional roles for men and women or in a power struggle which can be illustrated by a continuum with male dominance at one end, female dominance at the other. Since very few today would espouse either extreme, the ideal is perceived to be more or less toward the middle. Equality is seen as a midpoint between two extremes (see Figure 2).

```
MALE DOMINANCE                    FEMALE DOMINANCE
_____X_____
                    EQUALITY
```

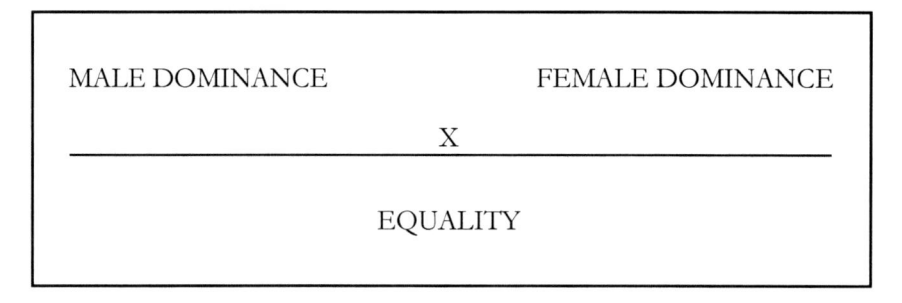

Figure 2

The words often used when talking about this continuum are: authority, command, power, mastery, reign, rule. Authority is seen as authority "over" someone else who must be submissive to that authority.

The problem with this model is that it is a power-based model and to discuss the role of women within this model simply perpetuates that power struggle. Some try to move the point of balance from the male dominance end toward the center point, or even try to counterbalance the male dominance by moving the balance point to the female dominance side of the continuum.

But, no matter where you agree to place the balance point on this continuum, the position can only be maintained by tension between the two opposing ends. If one gives a little, the other gains a little. If one gains a little, the other loses a little. Thus men and women are set in an adversarial position, and no matter where you decide the ideal point should be, it can only be maintained by resisting the encroachment of the other's power. Men then fear encouraging the "power" of women and women resist the "power" of men.

As long as the church uses this model and attempts to find the balance between the dominance of men and the dominance of women, tension persists. Tension is created by fear: fear of the power of others; fear of one's own power; fear of being controlled; fear of losing control. Dominance always begets fear. But the message of Scripture has nothing to do with dominance. Rather, the message of Scripture is that life in the community of believers is characterized by a servant attitude. The goal is to build one another up in love within the body of Christ. A framework that fosters dominance rather than servanthood cannot be our model.

If, instead, the framework is that of redemption, the results of sin are seen as unwelcome and the need to redeem the effects of sin becomes our goal. That includes the dominance of the male - not to be replaced by the dominance of the female, nor even to be held in balance by tension between the two - but by entirely moving away from a dominance model and embracing the new model - the new order - which Christ, in love, came to establish.

What then, does a model look like that is created by love: that rejects dominance as unbiblical?

C. Accepting Jesus' Paradigm

In order to establish a Biblical model for the functioning of men and women in the body of Christ, we must move away from the continuum of dominance into another sphere entirely (see Figure 3). Service within the kingdom cannot be determined by a balance point between male and female dominance but must be based on the new order ushered in by Christ: the new community where the nurturing of life and the development of gifts rules out any dominance.

```
┌─────────────────────────────────────────────────┐
│              Continuum of Dominance              │
├─────────────────────────────────────────────────┤
│ Male Dominance                   Female Dominance│
│                                                  │
│                    ┌─Sphere─┐                    │
│                  →│   of    │                    │
│                    │Development│                  │
│                    └─────────┘                    │
│                                                  │
└─────────────────────────────────────────────────┘
```

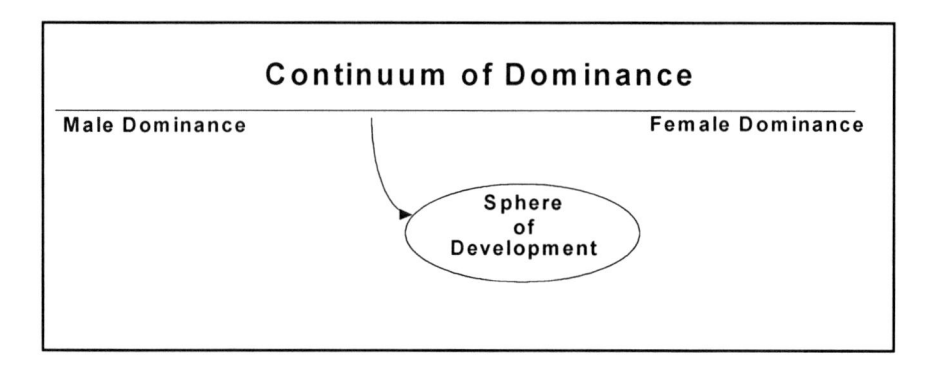

Figure 3

In this framework, questions are asked out of a different worldview and the continuum of authority, command, power, mastery, reign and rule gives way to the sphere of encouragement, nurturing and community. Instead of a power-based model, it is a gift-based model in which authority is not "over" but "on behalf of." Equality is not maintained by one giving up power to another, but is an inherent value of the community.

The words used in reference to this sphere are: gifts, service, encouragement, nurturing, community. Authority is placed in the word of God and positions of authority are given for the good of others, not in order to have power over others. Submission is seen as mutual submission to one another in the body and to Christ. Function flows out of spiritual giftedness rather than gender.

It was the redemptive act of Jesus, rather than the consequences of sin, that established this new framework and it is therefore imperative that we view all of Scripture through the "window" of that redemption.

This is the framework within which to look at the issue of women in the church.

Discussion and Reflection Questions

1. What model has governed your thinking and/or your discussions about the role of women in the church?

2. What model do you think Jesus would use?

3. Can you give examples of the power struggle illustrated in Figure 2?

4. Have you thought about the framework or lens you use to interpret the message of the Bible?

5. What differences do you see between reading Scripture through the paradigm of the Fall and reading that same Scripture through the paradigm of Redemption? For example, read Romans 5:12-19 from the perspective of the Fall - that God has ordained that we live under the reign of sin and death. Then read it again from the perspective of Redemption - that God has described the consequences of sin but has ordained that we are to be set free from the law of sin and death through the death and resurrection of Christ. What difference does the framework make in your interpretation? Try the same thing with Colossians 3:5-10.

6. What difference would it make to you if you lived on the continuum of dominance or in the sphere of development? Be as specific as you can.

7. What is the difference between authority "over" and authority "on behalf of" another? Give examples.

Chapter 3
INTERPRETING SCRIPTURE

The challenge here is to analyze the role of women through the paradigm of redemption

A. The Old Testament

1. Creation

Genesis 1:26-28

Then God said, "Let us make man in our image, in our likeness, and let them rule over the fish of the sea and the birds of the air, over the livestock, over all the earth, and over all the creatures that move along the ground." So God created man (adamah) in his own image, in the image of God he created him; male and female he created them. God blessed them and said to them, "Be fruitful and increase in number; fill the earth and subdue it. Rule over the fish of the sea and the birds of the air and over every living creature that moves on the ground.

Many people look to the order of creation (man created before woman) as the model or standard by which we are to determine the functions of women within the church and home. The difficulty is that there is confusion about what the creation story actually tells us regarding God's intended plan for male and female relationships.

The confusion results from our tendency to read into Scripture what we have been taught it says rather than approach Scripture free of bias and let it speak to us.

Let us take a fresh look at the creation story.

In this initial account of creation (as in all passages), we need to look for what is told to us <u>in</u> the text, not for what we choose to read <u>into</u> the text.

First, the use of *adam* can be confusing. God said, "Let us make *adam* (which sounds like the Hebrew for ground *adamah*) in our image...and let them rule." Here *adam* clearly is plural and must refer to humanity - male and female.

Next, it is clear that the command to rule over the earth is given to THEM - male and female. It is not given to the male with the female as his assistant, servant, slave, or subordinate. Nor was this command given to the male before the female was created - so the idea of the female being created as a subordinate "helper" for the man to rule the earth does not come from this text.

The female is made in the image of God just as much as the male. God blessed them together, as male and female, commanded them to fulfill the earth and subdue it and to have dominion over all created life. They were to share humanity, and to jointly participate in the blessings and the responsibilities. Genesis 1, therefore, argues against the inferiority or the subordination of woman.

This passage also refutes the concept that sex and sexuality are the result of sin since God created humanity as male and female before sin entered into the world.

Genesis 1 acts as a prologue giving an overview of the whole creation; whereas Genesis 2 focuses in on the sixth day of creation giving more information about the creation of humanity as male and female.

2. Expanded Story of Creation

Genesis 2:7-25

The Lord God formed the man from the dust of the ground and breathed into his nostrils the breath of life, and the man became a living being.

Now the Lord God had planted a garden in the east, in Eden; and there he put the man he had formed. And the Lord God made all kinds of trees grow out of the ground--trees that were pleasing to the eye and good for food. In the middle of the garden were the tree of life and the tree of the knowledge of good and evil....

The Lord God took the man and put him in the Garden of Eden to work it and take care of it. And the Lord God commanded the man, "You are free to eat from any tree in the garden; but you must not eat from the tree of the knowledge of good and evil, for when you eat of it you will surely die." The Lord God said, "It is not good for the man to be alone. I will make a helper suitable for him."

Now the Lord God had formed out of the ground all the beasts of the field and all the birds of the air. He brought them to the man to see what he would name them; and whatever the man called each living creature, that was its name.

So the man gave names to all the livestock, the birds of the air and all the beasts of the field. But for Adam (or the man) no suitable helper was found. So the Lord God caused the man to fall into a deep sleep; and while he was sleeping, he took one of the man's ribs (or took part of the man's side) and closed up the place with flesh. Then the Lord God made a woman from the rib (or part) he had taken out of the man, and he brought her to the man.

The man said, "This is now bone of my bones and flesh of my flesh; she shall be called 'woman' for she was taken out of man." For this reason a man will leave his father and mother and be united (cleave) to his wife, and they will become one flesh. The man and his wife were both naked, and they felt no shame.

Genesis 2 gives an expanded account of the creation of male and female and it is from this text that some would argue for male superiority and female subordination. The main arguments used to support this position include the idea that the first-born has both preeminence and authority; that a helper is subordinate; and that naming implies authority. But a careful analysis of those arguments proves them inconclusive.

Does being created first give authority?

The suggestion that being created first equals authority is again a concept that is read into the text. There is no hierarchy suggested in this text - only incompleteness. The idea that because man was created first means that the male is superior is an idea superimposed on the text, not found in it.

Does "helper" mean "subordinate"?

Another reason some argue for male authority from this passage is because of the use of the words *'ezer knegdo* which are translated "helper suitable" for him.

There has traditionally been a great emphasis on the use of "helper" or "helpmate" as an argument for God's intention of hierarchy; however, a careful study of the Hebrew words *'ezer knegdo* clearly dispels that idea.

The use of the English word "helper" suggests a subordinate or an inferior whereas the Hebrew word *'ezer* carries no such connotation. The word *'ezer* (helper) which here describes the woman, refers to God in 15 of the 21 times it is used in the Old Testament where its meaning is that of "protector" (Psalm 33:20) and "rescuer," (Exodus 18:4). This clearly precludes the idea that *'ezer* inherently carries a sense of inferior status.[1] In fact, by describing God as the superior who creates, protects and rescues Israel it could suggest "superiority" rather than "subordination," except for the fact that when it refers to the woman, it is modified by the word *knegdo* which means "face to face," "equivalent to," "in front of," or "visible." As Phyllis Trible explains in *God and the Rhetoric of Sexuality*, it is this modifier which "tempers this connotation of superiority to specify identity, mutuality, and equality. According to Yahweh God, what the earth creature needs is a companion who is neither subordinate nor superior: one who alleviates isolation through identity."[2]

What is presented here, then, is a mirror image which rules out either authority or subordination. Similarity is what is important. Unfortunately the concept that is still being read into this text by many people is the idea that "helper" implies subordination.

J.I. Packer, in an article, "I Believe in Women's Ministry" uses the idea of the woman being the helper to suggest that man is always the initiator and leader; that woman always comes alongside but never initiates.[3] She can have no responsibility nor authority over men. But again this is a concept attributed to the word "helper" which does not come from the normal usage of the original Hebrew word *'ezer*.

Aida Besancon Spencer in *Beyond the Curse* clarifies this issue when she says that," "To denigrate the term 'helper' is to ignore the total context of Genesis 2. Woman was created not to serve Adam, but to serve with Adam"[4] Adam was put into the garden of Eden to "work it and take care of it" (Genesis 2:15) and God said that it was not good for him to be alone.

"Alone" speaks of being in isolation instead of in relationship. Man needs woman, not because he cannot till the garden alone, but because he is relational and cannot give full expression to his human nature (made in the image of God) without an '*ezer knegdo* - someone like himself worthy of receiving his love and able to give him love - someone who is his equal, his partner, his "face-to-face" companion. It is not because of their difference that man needs woman but rather because they are alike and humanity was created to be relational.[5]

When God presents the animals to Adam, the man names them and the discovery is made that none of them is suitable as the helper equal to him - until God creates woman. There is nothing in the text to suggest that their tasks will be different - simply that the man needed a helper that was suitable - that together they would fulfill the command of Genesis 1. "To till and to guard" the garden is one way in which humans "rule over all the earth."[6]

Does naming give authority?

The idea that the man demonstrated his authority over the animals by naming them and so demonstrated his authority over the woman by naming **her** is an example of using the Fall as the framework which controls all of Scripture since Eve is actually not named until after the fall (Genesis 3:20). The naming of Eve cannot therefore be used as a basis for God ordaining male authority in creation.

Of perhaps greater significance is the fact that this interpretation misses the whole point of the story, which is the declaration that male and female are of the same essence.

The fact that woman was created from man does not make her subordinate any more than man is subordinate to the earth because he was taken from the earth. Instead, what the text points out is that the essence of her identity is "the same as" the male rather than "different from" the male. The text clearly states that the woman was "flesh of my flesh and bone of my bones." Male and female are "one flesh" - two of the same kind - unlike the animals.

As each animal is brought to the man, he gives it a name that is not related to his own - their essence is different. But when the woman is brought to him he recognizes her as having come from him. She is of the same essence and humanity is now identified as male and female: *ish* and *isshah*. The emphasis is on the unity - the same substance - as opposed to the animals. One is the derivation of the other.

A careful reading of the text reveals that the naming of Eve cannot be used to support the authority of the male over the female. Any concept of authority comes only from reading **into** the text a meaning that has been determined beforehand.

Who cleaves to whom?

In addition to refuting the traditional idea that male authority is established in creation, the Genesis account presents an unusual picture: the male is to leave his parents and cleave to his wife (King James Version). This is contrary to a patriarchal view of male and female relationships which would expect the female to leave her home and cleave to the male. The New International Version of the

Bible translates the Hebrew word *dabaq* in Genesis 2:24 as "be united with" (see quoted text p.21) whereas in other passages the same word is translated "hold fast to" which is closer to the Hebrew meaning.[7] As Mary Evans concludes in *Woman in the Bible*, the word "cleave" in the Hebrew text refers to the weaker one cleaving to the stronger.[8] It is the picture of Israel cleaving to God (Deuteronomy 10:20; Joshua 23:8), not vice versa.

Summary

The first chapter of Genesis clearly indicates that woman comes from the same source as man. She is created by the will of God, in the image of God. Chapter two stresses that the woman and the man have the same relationship and function. Each is dependent on the other as together, in unity, they enjoy both the blessings and the responsibilities of procreation and dominion.

The emphasis here is not on how they were created, but how they were related.[9] They identified with each other without shame. This was the beginning of community.

It is clear, then, that the introduction to the Biblical story presents the "creation order" in which male and female are created as equals in the image of God, equally called into a relationship with their creator and equally mandated to have dominion over the created order. There is nothing within these two chapters to denote hierarchy, subordination, patriarchy, or even submission. These concepts are found there only when they are read **into** the text by a predetermined interpretation.

3. Relationship Spoiled by Sin

Some feminists say that Genesis 3:16 (see bold text below) is the foundation of women's subjugation and must be rejected. Traditionalists say this is the basis for male authority and female subordination which is permanent and normative.

How are we to view this passage? What really took place? Adam and Eve had been created for unity: they were of the same essence, created for the same purpose. They were both created in the image of God, and were together to exercise responsibility for the created order.

When sin entered, two things happened on the human level: the unity they had known was disrupted - they hid from God and from each other by covering their nakedness with fig leaves; and the mutual responsibility they were given vanished and blame took its place. The result was that one became ruler, the other subject. The result of sin was a disruption of the community God intended for humanity.

Genesis 3:1-24

Now the serpent was more crafty than any of the wild animals the Lord God had made. He said to the woman, "Did God really say, 'You must not eat from any tree in the garden'?" The woman said to the serpent, "We may eat fruit from the trees in the garden, but God did say, 'You must not eat fruit from the tree that is in the middle of the garden, and you must not touch it, or you will die.'" "You will not surely die," the serpent said to the woman. "For God knows that when you eat of it your eyes will be opened, and you will be like God, knowing good and evil." When the woman saw that the fruit of the tree was good for food and pleasing to the eye, and also desirable for gaining wisdom, she took some and ate it. She also gave some to her husband, who was with her, and he ate it. Then the eyes of both of them were opened, and they realized they were naked; so they sewed fig leaves together and made coverings for themselves.

Then the man and his wife heard the sound of the Lord God as he was walking in the garden in the cool of the day, and they hid from the Lord God among the trees of the garden. But the Lord God called to the man, "Where are you?" He answered, "I heard you in the garden, and I was afraid because I was naked; so I hid." And he said, "Who told you that you were naked? Have you eaten from the tree that I commanded you not to eat from?" The man said, "The woman you put here with me--she gave me some fruit from the tree, and I ate it." Then the Lord God said to the woman, "What is this you have done?" The woman said, "The serpent deceived me, and I ate." So the Lord God said to the serpent, "Because you have done this, Cursed are you above all the livestock and all the wild animals! You will crawl on your belly and you will eat dust all the days of your life. And I will put enmity between you and the woman, and between your offspring (or seed) and hers; he will crush (or strike) your head, and you will strike his heel."

To the woman he said, "I will greatly increase your pains in childbearing; with pain you will give birth to children. Your desire will be for your husband, and he will rule over you."

To Adam he said, "Because you listened to your wife and ate from the tree about which I commanded you, 'You must not eat of it,'

"Cursed is the ground because of you; through painful toil you will eat of it all the days of your life. It will produce thorns and thistles for you, and you will eat the plants of the field. By the sweat of your brow you will eat your food until you return to the ground, since from it you were taken; for dust you are and to dust you will return."

Adam (or the man) named his wife Eve because she would become the mother of all the living. The Lord God made garments of skin for Adam and his wife and clothed them. And the Lord God said, "The man has now become like one of us, knowing good and evil. **He must not be allowed to reach out his hand and take also from the tree of life and eat, and live forever." So the Lord God banished him from the Garden of Eden to work the ground from which he had been taken.**

After he drove the man out, he placed on the east side of the Garden of Eden cherubim and a flaming sword flashing back and forth to guard the way to the tree of life.

George Knight III, who believes in a hierarchical relationship between male and female, states in *The New Testament Teaching on the Role Relationship of Men and Women* that Genesis 3 presumes that the role relationship between wife and husband has been established by God's creation order, a relationship that will now experience the effects of sin. He claims that the phrase, "He shall rule over you," expresses the effects of sin corrupting [their] relationship.[10] In this he is accurate. Where he is mistaken is firstly by presuming that the relationship ordained by God in the creation story is one of hierarchy, and secondly by the way in which that relationship was corrupted.

Knight claims that the relationship created by God is that of husband as head (meaning the one in authority) and the wife as helper (meaning subordinate to his authority). The result of sin then, according to Knight, is to make her unwilling to submit to his authority.[11]

The fallacy in this argument is that the relationship God established was not one of authority and subordination. It is true that sin corrupted the relationship - but the corruption was to MAKE it one of authority - one of dominance and subservience. Prior to their disobedience the male and female were "one flesh" by derivation and by action (Gen. 2:24). But now the "one flesh" is divided. In the words of Phyllis Trible:

> The man will not reciprocate the woman's desire; instead, he will rule over her....Hence the woman is corrupted into becoming a slave and the man is corrupted into being a master. His supremacy is neither a divine right nor a male prerogative. Her subordination is neither a divine decree nor the female destiny. God describes this consequence but does not prescribe it as punishment.[12]

Although patriarchy is a social system which is not necessarily anti-women, it can legitimize the power of a male-dominated society to subjugate and exploit women. In the patriarchal Hebrew society, God instructed his people to witness to His redemptive power by acting fairly and compassionately toward anyone in their power.[13] According to Gretchen Gaebelin Hull

> as we contemplate the social system of patriarchalism, the real question is not how best to patch up a system that legitimizes discrimination and abuses of human rights, but whether we should patch it up at all.[14]

Hull claims that God's redemptive power should cause us to shrink from any philosophy that says, "One person must always be dominant" and see that to "Christianize" such a philosophy is to end it.[15]

It is important to note that neither the male nor the female is cursed: only the serpent and the ground (see bold text above). While the consequences of sin for the woman include pain in childbirth and desire for her husband that allows him to dominate, and for the man, toil in producing food and banishment from the garden; they are not, however, intended to be permanent but are redeemable in the same way that all the consequences of sin are - through the common grace of God in the discoveries of science, medicine and compassionate human activity, and through the shed blood of Jesus. Jesus came to take away the effects of the fall and certainly mankind has co-operated in negating the toil - both in producing food and children. Should not women also benefit from the negation of male "rulership" and instead enjoy "relationships of equality...[living] lives affected by Christ's redemption."[16]

4. The Female in the Old Testament

Female Imagery for God

God is portrayed as providing food, water, and clothing - functions carried out by the women in Hebrew culture. God is also described as one who experiences birth pangs, nurses a child, comforts like a mother and experiences the emotions usually attributed to mothers. God is also the one who wipes away all tears.

> ***Isaiah 66:13*** *As a mother comforts her child, so will I comfort you; and you will be comforted over Jerusalem.*
>
> ***Genesis 3:21*** *The Lord God made garments of skin for Adam and his wife and clothed them.*
>
> ***Isaiah 42:14*** *For a long time I have kept silent, I have been quiet and held myself back. But now, like a woman in childbirth, I cry out, I gasp and pant.*

> ***Job 38:8-9*** *Who shut up the sea behind doors when it burst forth from the womb, when I made the clouds its garment and wrapped it in thick darkness.*
>
> ***Isaiah 49:13-15*** *Shout for joy, O heavens; rejoice, O earth; burst into song, O mountains! For the Lord comforts his people and will have compassion on his afflicted ones. But Zion said, "The Lord has forsaken me, the Lord has forgotten me." "Can a mother forget the baby at her breast and have no compassion on the child she has borne? Though she may forget, I will not forget you!*

Since goddess worship was strictly forbidden for the Hebrews, it is surprising that the female images of God have been recorded; however, female images of God do not mean that God is female. Neither do male images of God mean that God is male. Any reference to God as male or female is at variance with the Hebrew understanding of Yahweh. All images, whether male or female, are metaphysical and function not to sexualize but to personalize God and to demonstrate how God acts in relationship to the creation. Sexuality and therefore "maleness" is a characteristic of the created world.

Some Christians, in order to maintain and support the concept of male authority, make a subtle shift in language. They would agree that God is not male (a sexual designation), but claim that He is masculine (a behavioural designation). The implications of that shift are significant for women. If God is masculine, then it is clear that male behaviour more nearly reflects the image of God in the world, a fact which makes the "differentness between men and women [assume] a new level of significance, one that goes beyond biological and social differences and enters the spiritual."[17]

The Bible, however, provides no absolute and exclusive classification of masculine and feminine behaviour, speaking only of men and women, (as male and female,) who are to be conformed to the image of Christ. Sexuality is something that God created for humans. The Old Testament staunchly refuses to attribute sexuality or sexual activity to Yahweh. It is a "teaching from ancient pagan religions which saw the primal creative force as sexual in nature."[18] The Bible teaches that the earth and its people were created by the will of God. God spoke the world into being and then he took the substance of his created world to form human life. This is an act of creation, not reproduction. "God created - not procreated - the world and its inhabitants."[19]

Roles of Women in the Old Testament

Women held every office except Priest in Hebrew society. The leadership of women came through the offices of Judge, Queen, and Prophet:

Judge: Judges 4:4-16

Deborah, a prophetess, the wife of Lappidoth, was leading Israel at that time....and the Israelites came to her to have their disputes decided. She sent for Barak son of Abinoam from Kedesh in Naphtali and said to him, "The Lord, the God of Israel, commands you: 'Go, take with you ten thousand men of Naphtali and Zebulun and lead the way to Mount Tabor. I will lure Sisera, the commander of Jabin's army, with his chariots and his troops to the Kishon River and give him into your hands.'" Barak said to her, "If you go with me, I will go; but if you don't go with me, I won't go." "Very well," Deborah said, "I will go with you. But because of the way you are going about this, the honor will not be yours, for the Lord will hand Sisera over to a woman." So Deborah went with Barak to Kedesh....Sisera gathered together his nine hundred iron chariots and all the men with him, from Harosheth Haggoyim to the Kishon River. Then Deborah said to Barak, "Go! This is the day the Lord has given Sisera into your hands. Has not the Lord gone ahead of you?" So Barak went down Mount Tabor, followed by ten thousand men. At Barak's advance, the Lord routed Sisera and all his chariots and army by the sword, and Sisera abandoned his chariot and fled on foot. But Barak pursued the chariots and army as far as Harosheth Haggoyim. All the troops of Sisera fell by the sword; not a man was left.

Before Israel had kings, God appointed judges to rule. They "administered God's justice and pointed to Israel's ultimate Deliverer."[20] This passage describes Deborah not only as a judge but also as a prophetess and asserts that she "was leading Israel at that time."

God spoke through her to Barak, who was prepared to go into battle only if Deborah went with him. The final statement about her rule was that "peace reigned in the land for forty years" (Judges 5:31).

Queen: 2 Kings 11:1-16

> *When Athaliah the mother of Ahaziah saw that her son was dead, she proceeded to destroy the whole royal family. But Jehosheba, the daughter of King Jehoram and sister of Ahaziah, took Joash son of Ahaziah and stole him away from among the royal princes, who were about to be murdered. She put him and his nurse in a bedroom to hide him from Athaliah; so he was not killed. He remained hidden with his nurse at the temple of the Lord for six years while Athaliah ruled the land. In the seventh year Jehoiada sent for the commanders of units of a hundred, the Carites and the guards and had them brought to him at the temple of the Lord. He made a covenant with them and put them under oath at the temple of the Lord....Jehoiada brought out the king's son and put the crown on him; he presented him with a copy of the covenant and proclaimed him king. They anointed him, and the people clapped their hands and shouted, "Long live the king!" When Athaliah heard the noise made by the guards and the people, she went to the people at the temple of the Lord. She looked and there was the king, standing by the pillar, as the custom was. The officers and the trumpeters were beside the king, and all the people of the land were rejoicing and blowing trumpets. Then Athaliah tore her robes and called out, "Treason! Treason!" Jehoiada the priest ordered the commanders of units of a hundred, who were in charge of the troops: "Bring her out between the ranks and put to the sword anyone who follows her." For the priest had said, "She must not be put to death in the temple of the Lord." So they seized her as she reached the place where the horses enter the palace grounds, and there she was put to death.*

On the death of her son and king, the dowager queen Athaliah took action to assure the throne of the Southern Kingdom for herself and completed a seven year reign. The fact that she was not godly but was power hungry, as were many of her male counterparts, does not negate the reality that the Israelites were ruled by a woman.

Prophet: 2 Kings 22:8-20

Hilkiah the high priest said to Shaphan the secretary, "I have found the Book of the Law in the temple of the Lord." He gave it to Shaphan, who read it....Then Shaphan the secretary informed the king, "Hilkiah the priest has given me a book." And Shaphan read from it in the presence of the king. When the king heard the words of the Book of the Law, he tore his robes. He gave these orders to Hilkiah the priest, Ahikam son of Shaphan, Acbor son of Micaiah, Shaphan the secretary and Asaiah the king's attendant: "Go and inquire of the Lord for me and for the people and for all Judah about what is written in this book that has been found. Great is the Lord's anger that burns against us because our fathers have not obeyed the words of this book; they have not acted in accordance with all that is written there concerning us."

Hilkiah the priest, Ahikam, Acbor, Shaphan and Asaiah went to speak to the prophetess Huldah, who was the wife of Shallum, son of Tikvah, the son of Harhas, keeper of the wardrobe. She lived in Jerusalem, in the Second District. She said to them, "This is what the Lord, the God of Israel, says: Tell the man who sent you to me, 'This is what the Lord says: I am going to bring disaster on this place and its people, according to everything written in the book the king of Judah has read. Because they have forsaken me and burned incense to other gods and provoked me to anger by all the idols their hands have made, my anger will burn against this place and will not be quenched.' Tell the king of Judah, who sent you to inquire of the Lord, 'This is what the Lord, the God of Israel, says concerning the words you heard: Because your heart was responsive and you humbled yourself before the Lord when you heard what I have spoken against this place and its people, that they would become accursed and laid waste, and because you tore your robes and wept in my presence, I have heard you, declares the Lord. Therefore I will gather you to your fathers, and you will be buried in peace. Your eyes will not see all the disaster I am going to bring on this place.'" So they took her answer back to the king.

After Hilkiah, the high priest, found the book of the law and advised Joash the king about the discovery, the king sent the priest and others to the prophetess, Huldah, to enquire about God's word for the nation. Huldah faithfully spoke God's message of judgment to the delegation.

> ***Prophet: Nehemiah 6:14***
>
> *Remember Tobiah and Sanballat, O my God, because of what they have done; remember also the prophetess Noadiah and the rest of the prophets who have been trying to intimidate me*

This passage adds Noadiah to the short list of women that the Old Testament recognizes as prophetesses: Miriam (Exodus 15:20); Deborah (Judges 4:4); and Huldah (2 Kings 22:14 and 2 Chronicles 34:22).

Song of Solomon

This Old Testament book clearly affirms the mutuality of the sexes. There is no male dominance, no female subordination, and no stereotyping[21] in the Song of Solomon.

The Ideal Wife

The ideal wife presented in Proverbs 31 is known to us as the virtuous woman or the "good wife" because that is what translators have given us. But, as Faith Martin points out, she is called *chayil* in Hebrew, a word that means 'valorous, strong and powerful.' When the Hebrew text applies *chayil* to men, English texts render it 'valor' or 'brave'...but when women are called *chayil* the same translators render the word 'good,' 'noble,' or 'virtuous.' "None of these words matches *chayil* in meaning or intensity: a strong woman - who can find her!"[22]

> ***Proverbs 31:10-31***
>
> *A wife of noble character who can find? She is worth far more than rubies.*
> *Her husband has full confidence in her and lacks nothing of value.*

She brings him good, not harm, all the days of her life.
She selects wool and flax and works with eager hands.
She is like the merchant ships, bringing her food from afar.
She gets up while it is still dark; she provides food for her family and portions for her servant girls.
She considers a field and buys it; out of her earnings she plants a vineyard.
She sets about her work vigorously; her arms are strong for her tasks.
She sees that her trading is profitable, and her lamp does not go out at night.
In her hand she holds the distaff and grasps the spindle with her fingers.
She opens her arms to the poor and extends her hands to the needy.
When it snows, she has no fear for her household; for all of them are clothed in scarlet.
She makes coverings for her bed; she is clothed in fine linen and purple.
Her husband is respected at the city gate, where he takes his seat among the elders of the land.
She makes linen garments and sells them, and supplies the merchants with sashes.
She is clothed with strength and dignity; she can laugh at the days to come.
She speaks with wisdom, and faithful instruction is on her tongue.
She watches over the affairs of her household and does not eat the bread of idleness.
Her children arise and call her blessed; her husband also, and he praises her:
"Many women do noble things, but you surpass them all."
Charm is deceptive, and beauty is fleeting; but a woman who fears the Lord is to be praised.
Give her the reward she has earned, and let her works bring her praise at the city gate.

The woman described here has property, provides for her husband and family, is generous, sells the goods she produces, speaks and teaches with wisdom, and is praised at the city gate - which is the place of the leaders.

Summary

The evidence is clear that women in the Old Testament, in spite of the fact that the general culture did not give them great respect outside the private sphere of their homes, nor permit much public opportunity for leadership, were called by God, gifted by God and set apart by God for specific tasks and their authority was recognized by the people. It is true that they were the exception but God does not make exceptions when his mandate is absolute. Today, the response to the role of women in the Old Testament varies. As Martin points out:

> Many Christians who believe in male authority cite the Old Testament way of life as God's ideal plan for society. The Patriarchy and the fatherhood of God are seen as compatible ideals, comfortable equivalents, with the result that the place of women in the Old Testament is seen as God's will for family life today. Secular feminists, on the other hand, seize on the injustice of woman's place in ancient society and ridicule God as just another male bully. They, too, assume that God designed the patriarchal system.[23]

However, "patriarchy was not peculiar to the Hebrew nation, but was the economic, legal, and social system of the known pagan world,"[24] and is not, therefore, a continued requirement for God's people.

5. Prophecy of a New Paradigm

Joel 2:28-29

And afterward, I will pour out my Spirit on all people. Your sons and daughters will prophesy, your old men will dream dreams, your young men will see visions. Even on my servants, both men and women, I will pour out my Spirit in those days. They will be his people, and God himself will be with them and be their God.

God revealed to Joel that there would come a time when His Spirit would be poured out on all believers, young and old, men and women. All believers would share equally in the outpouring of God's Spirit and in the prophesying which would be the result. This is the announcement of the new order and a new paradigm - that of redemption.

Discussion and Reflection Questions

1. What new thoughts do you have as a result of a fresh look at the creation stories?

2. If you had only Genesis 1 and 2 as biblical reference material, what would you conclude about the roles and relationships of men and women?

3. Does the creation account in Genesis support hierarchy?

4. What is the significance of both male and female being created in the image of God?

5. Since Adam didn't name Eve until after the fall, how can the belief that "naming means power over" be seen as evidence that God intended a hierarchy at creation?

6. Can there be any distinction between men and women in their relationship to God? Their service to God?

7. How can the rulership of the male over the female be inferred from the priority of Adam's creation?

8. How would you describe the first "community" before sin entered? After sin entered?

9. Given our language categories, how can the concept that God is not "male" be taught without falling into the trap of portraying God as female? How are the male images of God to function for us? Can the female images of God function in the same way? How do we maintain a clear message that God is not sexual: neither male nor female, but Spirit; and that sexuality (and procreation) is a characteristic of the creation not the Godhead?

10. The Hebrew God differs dramatically from the pagan gods who were very sexual beings. How would this fact have impacted the revelation of God? Is the term "Father" designed to denote maleness?

11. Do you think of God as male? Why or why not?

12. Who determines what characteristics (i.e. nurturing, teaching, strength, emotions, organizational ability, leadership, servanthood, submission, gentleness, vulnerability, martyrdom, etc.) are feminine or masculine? Are they Biblically determined or culturally developed?

13. To counter the image of God as male, various solutions have been offered:

    - Some would call God mother as well as father.
    - Some would eliminate all nouns that have a strictly male connotation i.e. King, Master, Lord, Son, Father.
    - Some would use nouns which in our culture are seen as feminine - nurturer, comforter, life-giver.
    - Some would eliminate all masculine pronouns, repeating the noun and using "Godself" instead of "himself."
    - Some would say that since God is revealed to us in male language we cannot change it.
    - Some would say there is no problem - that the problem lies with those who have a problem - that this is the way it has always been and always should be.
    - Some would say, "While it isn't a problem for me, I recognize that it IS for some and I will try to be sensitive."

    What would you say?

B. The New Paradigm of Redemption

1. The Cultural Setting

As we move into the New Testament period, it is helpful to remember that the women in Jesus' life would have been primarily rural and mostly Jewish. They would have been primarily socialized in the Jewish culture, although by this time, the Roman and Hellenistic influences were prevalent. They certainly would have "known their place." Women were to function in the private domain of the home, while the public sphere was reserved for males.

The evidence concerning Jewish women's roles in religion indicates that by and large the religious privileges and functions they had were those they could participate in at home. The biblical rules in Leviticus 15 and their rabbinic interpretations restricted a woman's participation in the Temple rituals. Further, certain views about propriety appear to have taken away her theoretical right to read the Scriptures in the synagogue even in Jesus' day.[1]

In *Biblical Affirmations of Women,* Leonard Swidler points out that "the heart of Judaism is the study and living of Torah - the law - and the differing status of men and women is expressed here quite explicitly, for women were all but forbidden to study the Scriptures (Torah)."[2] He quotes Rabbi Eliezer (Mishnah 3,4):

> Rather should the words of the Torah be burned than entrusted to a woman....Whoever teaches his daughter the Torah is like one who teaches her obscenity.[3]

Swidler goes on to say:

> Women were also grossly restricted in public prayer. It was not possible for them to be counted toward the number necessary for a quorum to form a congregation to worship communally. They were...classified with children and slaves, who

similarly did not qualify... [and] were not allowed to read aloud or perform any leading function.[4]

Rabbis did not speak to women in public nor greet their own wives, daughters or mothers.[5] A woman's function was to manage her household and to bear and raise children and, with very few exceptions, they were not allowed to divorce their husbands, although men were allowed to divorce their wives.

Although the rights of women were very limited, and the public sphere basically denied to them, they did have significant responsibility and influence within the home.[6] It is not clear, however, how much a woman was to teach or be taught the Torah, even in the home, since not only were they were exempt from studying Torah but "along with children and slaves were not obliged to recite the Shema, the morning prayer, nor prayers at meals." (Mishnah 3,3)[7]

Further confusion comes from the fact that the Rabbis differed in their statements. While many made very derogatory comments about women, Rabbi ben Azzai said that a man ought to give his daughter a knowledge of the law.[8] And Mishnah Nadarim 4.3 reads, "He may teach scripture to his sons and daughters."[9]

As Tucker and Liefeld point out in *Daughters of the Church,* women might "learn a great deal informally, as they did through synagogue teaching, but a woman would not on her own enter into an association with a rabbi to become his disciple."[10]

It was into this Jewish society with its ambivalent attitude toward women that Jesus stepped and revealed a new paradigm, with new values, new attitudes and new practices.

2. The Attitude Required

An appropriate place to begin the study of Jesus' teaching with regard to the role of women in the church is with the passage in Luke 22 which outlines his mandate for the attitude which was to govern true Christian leadership.

Luke 22:24-30

Also a dispute arose among them as to which of them was considered to be greatest. Jesus said to them, "The kings of the Gentiles lord it over them; and those who exercise authority over them call themselves Benefactors. But you are not to be like that. Instead, the greatest among you should be like the youngest, and the one who rules like the one who serves. For who is greater, the one who is at the table or the one who serves? Is it not the one who is at the table? But I am among you as one who serves. You are those who have stood by me in my trials. And I confer on you a kingdom, just as my Father conferred one on me, so that you may eat and drink at my table in my kingdom and sit on thrones, judging the twelve tribes of Israel".

In response to a dispute among the disciples, Jesus teaches that the new community is based on servanthood, not on authority. His followers are not to be like the Gentiles who use the excuse that they are benefactors to "lord it over others," but rather they are to truly serve one another.

The community of faith was to live by a different set of rules from those they observed around them. An attitude of humble servanthood was to characterize them.

With that as a frame for ministry, we can now turn to Jesus' teaching as it specifically relates to women.

3. The Teaching and Modeling of Jesus

Matthew 19:29 (Mark 10:29-30)

And everyone who has left houses or brothers or sisters or father or mother or children or fields for my sake will receive a hundred times as much and will inherit eternal life.

According to Jesus' value system, it costs as much to give up a sister as a brother. In His mind, leaving a sister was significant enough to mention. "Jesus saw women as persons of value and worth, not just as inferior or despised females."[11]

Matthew 26:6-13 (Mark 14:3-9; John 12:1-8)

> *While Jesus was in Bethany in the home of a man known as Simon the Leper, a woman came to him with an alabaster jar of very expensive perfume, which she poured on his head as he was reclining at the table. When the disciples saw this, they were indignant. "Why this waste?" they asked. "This perfume could have been sold at a high price and the money given to the poor." Aware of this, Jesus said to them, "Why are you bothering this woman? She has done a beautiful thing to me. The poor you will always have with you, but you will not always have me. When she poured this perfume on my body, she did it to prepare me for burial. I tell you the truth, wherever this gospel is preached throughout the world, what she has done will also be told, in memory of her."*

There is a great deal written about this passage, but one significant observation is that Jesus here rebukes the disciples for assuming their spiritual understanding was greater than Mary's.[12] Various authors have identified Mary as "the first to understand the meaning of the death of Jesus,"[13] and indicate that "the expensive perfume that she lavishly pours on Jesus is her way of preparing Jesus for his burial."[14]

(See further comments about this event at John 12:1-8.)

Mark 5:22-42

> *Then one of the synagogue rulers, named Jairus, came there. Seeing Jesus, he fell at his feet and pleaded earnestly with him, "My little daughter is dying. Please come and put your hands on her so that she will be healed and live." So Jesus went with him. A large crowd followed and pressed around him. And a woman was there who had been subject to bleeding for twelve years. She had suffered a great deal under the care of many doctors and had spent all she had, yet instead of getting better she grew worse. When she heard about Jesus, she came up behind him in the crowd and touched his cloak, because she thought, "If I just touch his clothes, I will be healed." Immediately her bleeding stopped and she felt in her body that*

she was freed from her suffering. At once Jesus realized that power had gone out from him. He turned around in the crowd and asked, "Who touched my clothes?" "You see the people crowding against you," his disciples answered, "and yet you can ask, 'Who touched me?'" But Jesus kept looking around to see who had done it. Then the woman, knowing what had happened to her, came and fell at his feet and, trembling with fear, told him the whole truth. He said to her, "Daughter, your faith has healed you. Go in peace and be freed from your suffering."

While Jesus was still speaking, some men came from the house of Jairus, the synagogue ruler. "Your daughter is dead," they said. "Why bother the teacher any more?" Ignoring what they said, Jesus told the synagogue ruler, "Don't be afraid; just believe." He did not let anyone follow him except Peter, James and John the brother of James. When they came to the home of the synagogue ruler, Jesus saw a commotion, with people crying and wailing loudly. He went in and said to them, "Why all this commotion and wailing? The child is not dead but asleep." But they laughed at him. After he put them all out, he took the child's father and mother and the disciples who were with him, and went in where the child was. He took her by the hand and said to her, "Talitha koum!" (which means, "Little girl I say to you, get up!"). Immediately the girl stood up and walked around (she was twelve years old). At this they were completely astonished. He gave strict orders not to let anyone know about this, and told them to give her something to eat.

Jesus violated the traditional Jewish code in these interactions. When a woman who was "unclean" touched him, he spoke to her, welcomed her, sent her away healed, and did not resort to the required ritual of proceeding to the temple to be cleansed himself. Instead, he continued on his way to raise another female, Jairus' daughter, from the dead. He gave dignity, honour and respect as well as innate value to women in a culture that gave them a very different message.

Mark 10:11-12

Anyone who divorces his wife and marries another woman commits adultery against her. And if she divorces her husband and marries another man, she commits adultery.

This statement of Jesus' would have been quite radical because adultery against a wife was unheard of in the time of Jesus and also because a man could divorce his wife but a woman could not divorce her husband. The rules governing divorce are set out clearly in Deuteronomy 24:1-4. Swidler says that, "Since in Israel the man possessed the women and not vice versa, the man could dis-possess, that is, divorce, the woman, but she could not divorce him."[15]

Luke 10:38-42

As Jesus and his disciples were on their way, he came to a village where a woman named Martha opened her home to him. She had a sister called Mary, who sat at the Lord's feet listening to what he said. But Martha was distracted by all the preparations that had to be made. She came to him and asked, "Lord, don't you care that my sister has left me to do the work by myself? Tell her to help me. "Martha, Martha," the Lord answered, "you are worried and upset about many things, but only one thing is needed. Mary has chosen what is better, and it will not be taken away from her."

A woman's sphere was primarily the home and she was 'to be protected against unchastity.' Consequently women were often treated as persons who had little edification to share in conversation and who had little preparation to withstand the temptations of public life.[16] But Jesus' interaction with Mary is in direct contrast to the prevailing attitudes. The tradition of the day did not permit women to study the Law but expected them to serve. The expression "to sit at someone's feet" was the posture of a student. When Mary sat at Jesus' feet instead of helping Martha serve when Martha obviously needed her, Jesus reversed the priorities:

In choosing between a woman's role in homemaking and a woman's role in education... Jesus has concluded that a woman's role as homemaker is not primary. Jesus has returned to that original injunction in Deuteronomy 31:12: "Men, women, children, and strangers are to learn to fear the Lord and do all the Lord commands."[17]

Luke 11:27-28

As Jesus was saying these things, a woman in the crowd called out, "Blessed is the mother who gave you birth and nursed you." He replied, "Blessed rather are those who hear the word of God and obey it."

The purpose of this passage is not to deny that his mother is blessed, but rather to change the reason for her blessedness from that of being a mother to that of being a believer.

According to Jesus, true blessedness is not a result of biological function but rather of spiritual choice. As Spencer points out:

> More blessed are those women who hear and do God's word than those who nurse the wisest of all teachers...and in [Jesus'] whole ministry he constantly stressed the importance of allegiance to His name over allegiance to one's family.[18]

Luke 13:10-17

On a Sabbath, Jesus was teaching in one of the synagogues, and a woman was there who had been crippled for eighteen years. She was bent over and could not straighten up at all. When Jesus saw her, he called her forward and said to her, "Woman, you are set free from your infirmity." Then he put his hands on her, and immediately she straightened up and praised God. Indignant because Jesus had healed on the Sabbath, the synagogue ruler said to the people, "There are six days for work. So come and be healed on those days, not on the Sabbath." The Lord answered him, "You hypocrites! Doesn't each of you on the Sabbath untie his ox or donkey from the stall and lead it out to give it water? Then should not this woman, a daughter of Abraham, whom Satan has kept bound for eighteen long years, be set free on the Sabbath day from what bound her?" When he said this, all his opponents were humiliated, but the people were delighted with all the wonderful things he was doing.

Jesus was outraged at the callousness of the ruler of the synagogue and upbraided him for thinking more highly of his traditions and animals than of the crippled woman, reminding him that she was no less a descendant of Abraham than the ruler himself.[19] The fact of her being seen, touched and healed must have brought incredible joy. Mary Evans comments on the additional significance of Jesus calling her, "Daughter of Abraham." "'Son of Abraham' was a commonly used title, particularly when the worth of a man as a member of the covenant community was being emphasized [but] the title 'Daughter of Abraham' is virtually unknown in Judaistic writings. It appears that Jesus deliberately chose this title to bring out the value placed on this woman."[20]

John 4:7-42

When a Samaritan woman came to draw water, Jesus said to her, "Will you give me a drink?" (His disciples had gone into the town to buy food.) The Samaritan woman said to him, "You are a Jew and I am a Samaritan woman. How can you ask me for a drink?" (For Jews do not associate with Samaritans.) Jesus answered her, "If you knew the gift of God and who it is that asks you for a drink, you would have asked him and he would have given you living water." "Sir," the woman said, "you have nothing to draw with and the well is deep. Where can you get this living water? Are you greater than our father Jacob, who gave us the well and drank from it himself, as did also his sons and his flocks and herds?" Jesus answered, "Everyone who drinks this water will be thirsty again, but whoever drinks the water I give him will never thirst. Indeed, the water I give him will become in him a spring of water welling up to eternal life."

The woman said to him, "Sir, give me this water so that I won't get thirsty and have to keep coming here to draw water." He told her, "Go, call your husband and come back."

"I have no husband" she replied. Jesus said to her, "You are right when you say you have no husband. The fact is, you have

had five husbands, and the man you now have is not your husband. What you have just said is quite true." "Sir," the woman said, "I can see that you are a prophet. Our fathers worshiped on this mountain, but you Jews claim that the place where we must worship is in Jerusalem." Jesus declared, "Believe me, woman, a time is coming when you will worship the Father neither on this mountain nor in Jerusalem. You Samaritans worship what you do not know; we worship what we do know, for salvation is from the Jews. Yet a time is coming and has now come when the true worshipers will worship the Father in spirit and truth, for they are the kind of worshipers the Father seeks. God is spirit, and his worshipers must worship in spirit and in truth." The woman said, "I know that Messiah" (called Christ) "is coming. When he comes, he will explain everything to us." Then Jesus declared, "I who speak to you am he." Just then his disciples returned and were surprised to find him talking with a woman. But no one asked, "What do you want?" or "Why are you talking with her?"

Then, leaving her water jar, the woman went back to the town and said to the people, "Come, see a man who told me everything I ever did. Could this be the Christ? They came out of the town and made their way toward him. Meanwhile his disciples urged him, "Rabbi eat something." But he said to them, "I have food to eat that you know nothing about." Then his disciples said to each other, "Could someone have brought him food?" "My food," said Jesus, "is to do the will of him who sent me and to finish his work. Many of the Samaritans from that town believed in him because of the woman's testimony "He told me everything I ever did." So when the Samaritans came to him, they urged him to stay with them, and he stayed two days. And because of his words many more became believers. They said to the woman, "We no longer believe just because of what you said; now we have heard for ourselves, and we know that this man really is the Savior of the world.

Jesus' longest recorded conversation with an individual takes place with a woman - a Samaritan. Jesus consistently treated the marginalized members of society - the lepers, the crippled, the blind and the women - with dignity and respect and in this instance, he breaks all the taboos by speaking to a woman who is a Samaritan and who living with a man who is not her husband. He saw the woman as "capable of spiritual discernment."[21] "In choosing [this woman] as his first evangelist, Jesus makes the point that the world's notions of acceptability are not determining factors for Christian ministry."[22]

John 11:5- 27

Jesus loved Martha and her sister and Lazarus. Yet when he heard that Lazarus was sick, he stayed where he was two more days....When Martha heard that Jesus was coming, she went out to meet him, but Mary stayed at home. "Lord," Martha said to Jesus, "If you had been here, my brother would not have died. But I know that even now God will give you whatever you ask." ...Jesus said to her, "I am the resurrection and the life. He who believes in me will live, even though he dies; and whoever lives and believes in me will never die. Do you believe this?" "Yes, Lord," she told him, "I believe that you are the Christ, the son of God, who was to come into the world."

In this passage, Martha, the sister more commonly known for being perturbed by Mary's lack of help with the household duties, gives evidence of her very clear understanding of Jesus' identity. Her statement is almost identical to that of Peter's. Most of us know that Peter declared, "You are the Christ, the son of God," (Matthew 16:16) and we are aware of Jesus' affirmation of Peter's faith, but few of us know or remember that Martha is recorded as having made the same faith statement.

John 12:1-8

Six days before the Passover, Jesus arrived at Bethany, where Lazarus lived, whom Jesus had raised from the dead. Here a dinner was given in Jesus' honor. Martha served, while Lazarus was among those reclining at the table with him. Then Mary took about a pint of pure nard, an expensive perfume; she poured it on Jesus' feet and wiped his feet with her hair. And the house was filled with the fragrance of the perfume.

But one of his disciples, Judas Iscariot, who was later to betray him, objected, "Why wasn't this perfume sold and the money given to the poor? It was worth a year's wages." He did not say this because he cared about the poor but because he was a thief;

> *as keeper of the money bag, he used to help himself to what was put into it. "Leave her alone," Jesus replied. "It was intended that she should save this perfume for the day of my burial. You will always have the poor among you, but you will not always have me."*

Six days before the Passover, Jesus paid a visit to Bethany, where we again find Mary at Jesus' feet, this time anointing them with perfume and wiping them with her own hair.[23] "Mary understood the true nature of Jesus' messiahship, a theological insight that Jesus' male disciples failed to grasp throughout his entire earthly ministry."[24] Swidler comments that "women did not eat with men when guests were present, nor, indeed, did they even enter the dining area."[25] And once again, Jesus defended Mary's action even though she had disregarded societal expectations and acted in a manner that may have been seen as unseemly.

Summary

Jesus' teaching and his interaction with women make it clear that we are to view the role of women and men in the church as one of nurture and development which is based on gifts and motivated by servanthood. Jesus ushered in a new era and his treatment of women is to be our model.

Jesus didn't stand with placards on the street corners proclaiming that women were humans, created every bit as much as men, in the image of God. He simply and quietly reversed the traditional view through his actions - actions that were in and of themselves shocking enough, or significant enough, that they were recorded.

All the actions of Jesus: interacting with Mary and Martha; touching the woman who was menstrually unclean; talking with the Samaritan woman at the well and receiving those to whom she witnessed; telling Mary at the tomb to go and tell her brothers (John 20:17); refusing to condemn the woman caught in adultery but turning the sin back on the men who would have stoned her, thus making them aware of their own sinfulness and need for forgiveness; using women in his parables (Matthew 25:1-13;Luke 15:8-10; Luke 18:1-8) all add up to a message of his high regard for women and his willingness to disregard the social conventions of the day in order to affirm the dignity, humanity and spirituality of women.

Jesus gave women the freedom to respond to Him and His message of grace and mercy with an outpouring of gratitude; freedom to express that gratitude in service to Him and to others; and freedom to exercise giftedness in that service.

4. The Fulfillment of Joel's Prophecy

Acts 2:16-18

This is what was spoken by the prophet Joel: "In the last days, God said, I will pour out my Spirit on all people. Your sons and daughters will prophesy, your young men will see visions, your old men will dream dreams. Even on my servants, both men and women, I will pour out my Spirit in those days and they will prophesy."

Although some would teach that only part of Joel's prophecy was fulfilled in the "church age" and that the prophesying of women alongside men would be reserved for the "kingdom age" or the last days, others would challenge that position. As Tucker and Liefeld say, "It is hard to conceive of any formulation that would state more clearly that the gift of God's Spirit and the ensuing prophetic ministry was now bestowed fully and equally on women as well as men."[26]

Peter himself distinctly affirms that the prophecy of Joel was fulfilled - that the Spirit was poured out on both men and women on the day of Pentecost - that together they would speak forth the word of the Lord or 'prophesy."

There are others who agree that women can prophesy but would maintain a difference between the kind of prophesying that women can do and what men can do by saying that the prophesying meant by Joel and by Peter was somehow different from the "preaching" that only men can do because it involves speaking "authoritatively" which women are not permitted to do. To argue this, is to strip "prophecy" of its usual meaning throughout Scripture which is always to speak a word from the Lord: the prophet was God's spokesperson.[27]

5. The Teaching of Paul

In contrast to the women in Jesus' life, the women in Paul's writings would have been mainly urban. Some were obviously wealthy and many would have been Gentiles whose only religious worship experience would have been in a pagan cult.

The synagogue was a Jewish rather than a Christian worship center and while many Christians continued to worship there, the primary worship center for Christians would have been the household. There would not, therefore, have been the distinct separation of church and home that we experience in many cultures today. Consequently, the shift that Paul makes in his letters, from addressing the worshiping community to addressing family relations, is a very natural one.

According to Bristow in What Paul Really Said About Women,

Paul carefully chose his words, deliberately avoiding those Greek terms that, if he had used them, would have communicated to his readers precisely what our English translations imply for us today...and therein lies one of the greatest ironies of Christian history: The words of Paul (as translated), instead of communicating a clear message calling for sexual equality, have become the primary source of authority for the deprecation of women.[28]

Bristow goes on to say that our traditional understanding of what Paul wrote has led to a double standard. He argues that:

> We have all fallen heir to the traditional interpretation of what the apostle Paul declared to be true about women. We also fall heir to the traditional double standard for the sexes....We were taught that women, according to the good apostle Paul are more prone to fall when tempted than are men. After all, just look at the example of Eve. On the other hand, we were taught that women, according to the double standard, are responsible for upholding sexual virtues. After all, boys will be boys, but girls must be ladies and must tell the boys when to behave. Now, one may wonder, if females are less resistant to temptation, why it is they who must tell males when enough is enough? We were also taught that women, according to Paul,

are to obey their husbands and to be subject to male leadership. On the other hand, we were taught that women according to the double standard, have the ultimate position of leadership. After all, the 'hand that rocks the cradle rules the world.' One may wonder, if women are less fit leaders than men, how mothers can teach their sons to be good leaders?[29]

This traditional teaching has led to various explanations: that Paul was inconsistent; that he was confused; that he compromised the gospel so as not to upset the social structures of his day; or that he gave a good line in public but in private revealed his own disdain for women.[30]

None of these explanations is satisfactory. Paul was a first century Jewish Pharisee who saw the value of women ministering (Rom. 16:1-2,7; Phil. 4:1-3) and stood against it only in specific situations where it endangered the gospel (1 Tim. 2:8-15).

Obviously, a fresh look at Paul's letters is warranted.

Scholars do not agree on the dating or even on the authenticity of the authorship of the letters attributed to Paul. For the purposes of this study, the following letters will be accepted without debate as coming from Paul and they will be looked at in the order given, accepting the following dates for the writing.

> **The Travel Letters**
> Galatians - written from Antioch AD 48
> 1 Thessalonians - written from Corinth AD 50
> 2 Thessalonians - written from Corinth AD 50
> 1 Corinthians - written from Ephesus AD 54-55
> 2 Corinthians - written from Ephesus AD 54-55
> Romans - written from Corinth early AD 57
>
> **The Captivity Letters**
> Colossians - written from Rome AD 60-61
> Ephesians - written from Rome AD 60-61
> Philemon - written from Rome AD 60-61
> Philippians - written from Rome AD 60-61
>
> **The Pastoral Letters**
> Titus - written from Ephesus after AD 62
> 1 Timothy - written from Macedonia after AD 62
> 2 Timothy - written from Rome AD 64-65

Figure 4

Galatians 3:27-29

For all of you who were baptized into Christ have been clothed with Christ. There is neither Jew nor Greek, slave nor free, male nor female, for you are all one in Christ Jesus. If you belong to Christ, then you are Abraham's seed, and heirs according to the promise.

This is thought to have been a baptismal creed in use in the early church which Paul has used to illustrate his point that all racial, gender and class barriers are broken down in Christ. Paul, contrary to what most people have concluded, saw the practical ramifications for the oneness of male and female. His point in Galatians 3:28 is that faith in Christ has brought "a new relationship to God and it is accompanied...by a new relationship of believers to one another...Jew and Greek, slave and free, male and female - which encompass all humanity."[31]

Some say that Paul is here referring to a spiritual reality only and his statement is not intended to affect our physical reality and that we should, therefore, not expect to see the fulfillment of this statement here on earth. However, the context of this passage argues against that position. As Roberta Hestenes has pointed out:

> Paul opposes Peter to his face because Peter's refusal to eat with the Judaizers had the very practical implication of dividing the "heirs." Paul is angry with Peter for maintaining the distinction. He fully expects his manifesto to be acted on in the real life here and now. Paul's major thrust was the Jew/Gentile division and he expended his energy in breaking down these barriers. He very clearly said that differences no longer define or limit.[32]

Our primary identity is not that of gender, race or social class, but that we are in Christ. Faith in Christ defines who we are and we are to enjoy both the blessings and responsibilities equally. Any prior distinctions are now unimportant: racial, social and gender barriers are gone.

F. F. Bruce says, "If a Gentile may exercise spiritual leadership in church as freely as Jew, or a slave as freely as a citizen, why not a woman as freely as a man?"[33]

As Kjesbo and Grenz explain:

> Paul voices his radical assertion of Christian equality in the context of a discussion about circumcision. In the Old Testament, this ritual, which was a specifically male rite, marked the Israelites as the covenant people of God. In the New Testament era, however, circumcision has been replaced by baptism, in which all believers - male or female - can participate...[thus destroying] the distinctions between persons which formerly were used to establish social hierarchies.[34]

In Christ the wall of division is broken down. The letter to the Galatians is not talking exclusively about our spiritual life but also about how we are living out our Christian life - declaring emphatically that all partitions have been broken down.

1 Corinthians 7:4

Now for the matters you wrote about: It is good for a man not to marry. But since there is so much immorality, each man should have his own wife and each woman her own husband. The husband should fulfill his marital duty to his wife and likewise the wife to her husband. The wife's body does not belong to her alone but also to her husband. In the same way, the husband's body does not belong to him alone but also to his wife. Do not deprive each other except by mutual consent and for a time so that you may devote yourselves to prayer. Then come together again so that Satan will not tempt you because of your lack of self-control. I say this as a concession not as a command. I wish that all men were as I am but each man has his own gift from God: one has this gift, another has that.

This text gives an illustration of a husband and wife together making a decision which affects them both. It begins with some radical teaching about conjugal rights. The message that the body of the wife belongs to the husband was nothing new, but to say, "likewise, in the same way, the body of the husband belongs to the wife" was to introduce something quite new. And then the application is made quite clear - that if they want to abstain from sexual relations, it is to be by mutual consent.

This negates the idea that one person necessarily has to make a decision when there is an impasse. If Paul taught that in the most intimate relationship between a man and woman, there could be mutual consent, he is certainly reinforcing the idea of decision making being a partnership rather than a hierarchy.

Gretchen Gaebelein Hull makes the statement that if there is difficulty about decision making in a marriage, the question needs to be asked, "How Christian is my marriage!" She suggests that the "one flesh" union mandates that the <u>one</u> who should be making the decision is the "two become one."[35]

1 Corinthians 11:2-16

I praise you for remembering me in everything and for holding to the teachings, just as I passed them on to you. Now I want you to realize that the head of every man is Christ, and the head of the woman is man, and the head of Christ is God. Every man who prays or prophesies with his head covered dishonors his head. And every woman who prays or prophesies with her head uncovered dishonors her head--it is just as though her head were shaved. If a woman does not cover her head, she should have her hair cut off; and if it is a disgrace for a woman to have her hair cut or shaved off, she should cover her head. A man ought not to cover his head,* since he is the image and glory of God; but the woman is the glory of man.

*Or Every man who prays or prophesies with long hair dishonors his head. And every woman who prays or prophesies with no covering of hair on her head dishonors her head--she is just like one of the "shorn women." If a woman has no covering, let her be for now with short hair, but since it is a disgrace for a woman to have her hair shorn or shaved, she should grow it again. A man ought not to have long hair.

For man did not come from woman, but woman from man; neither was man created for woman, but woman for man. For this reason, and because of the angels, the woman ought to have [a sign of] authority on her head. In the Lord, however, woman is not independent of man, nor is man independent of woman. For as woman came from man, so also man is born of woman. But everything comes from God. Judge for yourselves: Is it proper for a woman to pray to God with her head uncovered? Does not the very nature of things teach you that if a man has long hair, it is a disgrace to him, but that if a woman has long hair, it is her glory? For long hair is given to her [instead of a veil?] as a covering. If anyone wants to be contentious about this, we have no [such?] other practice nor do the churches of God.

It is important to remember that this passage, although frequently used to restrict women, is not about gender roles but rather about worship protocol.. "Paul was dealing with the question of order... not laying down a canon law for the church until the end of time."[36]

This text assumes that both men and women are exercising their gifts - the question under discussion is <u>how</u> they should do it. The context of this passage is that Spiritual gifts were to be used <u>in</u> love and <u>for</u> unity.

However, when looking at the role of women in this passage, three issues need clarification:

1. What is the meaning of "head"?

2. Who has authority over what or whom?

3. What does "glory" signify?

The reference to angels is interesting but any attempt at interpretation is simply speculation.

What is the meaning of "head?"

The Greek word for "head," *kephale* appears 13 times in this passage and the question of interpretation centers around whether "head" implies authority or refers to source.

Western physiology suggests that "head" means the "boss" because of the fact that the brain controls the body. Martin claims, however, that the Greek understanding of physiology was different. "They believed that the heart was the seat of the intellect and the head was the source of life and life fluids.... Accordingly, when Zeus gave birth to [Athena, she] sprang from his head. A father was called the head of his child, meaning the father was the source of the child's life."[37]

Gilbert Bilezikian claims that *kephale* is always used "with the notion of serving the body in a creational, nurturing or representational dimension."[38]

> As head of the Church in Ephesians 1:22-23, Christ supplies the Body with its fullness....The issue is shared life. Christ fills the body. He is the source of life, the one who brings it to fullness or completion. The Body, in turn, is the expression of that fullness.[39]

Other passages which clearly define *kephale* as source of life and nurture are Ephesians 5:21-33 and Colossians 1:15-20. "Christ's headship to the church is paralleled to His love, care and nurture for the church....The Church finds its beginning in Him, the head. It started with Him, the firstborn. He is the source - the inception - of its existence."[40]

Traditionalists, as exemplified by James Hurley who wrote *Man and Woman in Biblical Perspective,* make the opposite claim that head *(kephale)* must mean authority.[41] A hermeneutical principle, however, is that when a word has more than one meaning, the correct one is determined from within the text - not brought to it. In this case, the context clearly indicates the meaning of source or origin: "man does not originate from woman, but woman from man." Paul is talking about creation in verse 9 *(neither was man created for woman, but woman for man)* and also in verse 12 *(for as woman came from man)*. He brings it all into perspective in that same verse, however, by pointing out our interdependence *(so also man is born of woman)* and he then culminates his argument by saying that everything originates from God *(but everything comes from God)*.

Another point in favour of understanding *kephale* as "source" is the fact that when the Hebrew word for "head" meant rule or authority, the translators of the Septuagint used the Greek word *archon*, rather than *kephale*, indicating that *kephale* was not the usual word for "authority" in the Greek.

Paul's understanding, therefore, of the metaphor (and almost certainly the only one the Corinthians would have grasped) is "head" as "source," especially "source of life."[42]

Who has authority over what?

James Hurley uses 1 Corinthians 11:7 to support his theory that women lack authority. He says that, "In [this] particular sense of authority relationships... it is absolutely appropriate to say that the man images God and that the woman does not."[43]

Many traditionalists would agree with Hurley and claim that this passage affirms man's authority over women. However, authority is mentioned only once and this single reference is to the woman's authority over her own head."[44] The word *exousia* in verse 10 means to HAVE authority, not to be UNDER authority. The syntax of this is such that it could be read to say either that women had the right to speak if they had a covering or that they had the right to decide if they would wear a covering or not."[45]

In many translations, the words "a sign of" have been added, perhaps to make sense to those translators who had predetermined that the text could not be saying what it in fact was saying: simply that the woman ought to have authority on her head.

Note the various translations:

> *NIV the woman ought to have a <u>sign of authority</u> on her head*
>
> *RSV a woman ought to have a <u>veil</u> on her head.*
>
> *KJV the woman ought to have <u>power</u> on her head*

The underlined words are all translations of the same word, *exousia*, which means authority, jurisdiction, liberty, power, might and strength. In the original Greek, Paul wrote that a woman had power or rights with regard to her head. "The only authority mentioned is the authority of the woman."[46] Exactly what that means is debatable, but what it certainly CANNOT mean is that the man is to have authority over her.

(See also comments on Ephesians 1:10, 1:22-23, 4:15-16 and 5:21-33.)

In what way is woman the glory of man?

Anne Atkins in her treatment of this subject in *Split Image*, indicates that in verses 9 and 12, Paul is referring to Genesis 2 so that in this passage:

> man stands for the whole human race; his very name means 'Humankind.' It is in this sense that he is God's glory. [Humankind] is His representative on earth, and the crown of his creation.[47]

She continues to explain that, as such, humanity is the "glory" of God - reflecting back to Him the truth of who God is. In the same way, the woman when she was created was a mirror, reflecting back to the male the glory - the true image - of who he was.

Only another human could do that: bone of my bone and flesh of my flesh. The woman was of the same essence as the man, bringing him honour and renown by reflecting back to him his identity as a relational being made in the image of God. To make her subordinate to him is to distort the meaning of "glory."

1 Corinthians 12:1-27

Now about spiritual gifts, brothers, I do not want you to be ignorant....There are different kinds of gifts, but the same Spirit. There are different kinds of service, but the same Lord. There are different kinds of working, but the same God works all of them in all men. Now to each one the manifestation of the Spirit is given for the common good. To one there is given through the Spirit the message of wisdom, to another the message of knowledge by means of the same Spirit, to another faith by the same Spirit, to another gifts of healing by that one Spirit, to another miraculous powers, to another prophecy, to another distinguishing between spirits, to another speaking in different kinds of tongues, and to still another the interpretation of tongues. All these are the work of one and the same Spirit, and he gives them to each one, just as he determines. The body is a unit, though it is made up of many parts; and though all its parts are many, they form one body. So it is with Christ. For we were all baptized by one Spirit into one body--whether Jews or Greeks, slave or free--and we were all given the one Spirit to drink. Now the body is not made up of one part but of many. If the foot should say, "Because I am not a hand, I do not belong to the body," it would not for that reason cease to be part of the body. And if the ear should say, "Because I am not an eye, I do not belong to the body," it would not for that reason cease to be part of the body. If the whole body were an eye, where would the sense of hearing be? If the whole body were an ear, where would the sense of smell be? But in fact God has arranged the parts in the body, every one of them, just as he wanted them to be. If they were all one part, where would the body be? As it is, there are many parts, but one body. The eye cannot say to the hand, "I don't need you!" And the head cannot say to the feet, "I don't need you!".... Now you are the body of Christ, and each one of you is a part of it.

All the passages which speak of the gifting of the Holy Spirit make it quite clear that giftedness was intended for the building up of the church and was not gender based. Grenz explains that those who would deny women positions of authority over men, create an artificial distinction between "gift" and "role." They are willing to admit that gifts are given to women but claim that their role is limited by their gender. The basis for this distinction is an appeal to the principle of female subordination, which, they claim, God established at creation.

In contrast, Grenz argues that:

> Even if God had built this principle into creation (which he did not), it would not necessarily require that the church continue to practice male leadership and female subordination. Christ did not establish the church simply to be the mirror of original creation but to be the eschatalogical new community, living in accordance with the principles of God's new creation and thereby reflecting the character of the triune God.[48]

1 Corinthians 14:26-40

When you come together, everyone has a hymn, or a word of instruction, a revelation, a tongue or an interpretation. All of these must be done for the strengthening of the church. If anyone speaks in a tongue, two--or at the most three--should speak, one at a time, and someone must interpret. If there is no interpreter, the speaker should keep quiet in the church and speak to himself and God. Two or three prophets should speak, and the others should weigh carefully what is said. And if a revelation comes to someone who is sitting down, the first speaker should stop. For you can all prophesy in turn so that everyone may be instructed and encouraged. The spirits of prophets are subject to the control of prophets. For God is not a God of disorder but of peace. As in all the congregations of the saints, women should remain silent in the churches. They are not allowed to speak, but must be in submission, as the Law says. If they want to inquire about something, they should ask their own husbands at home; for it is disgraceful for a woman to speak in the church.

Did the word of God originate with you? Or are you the only people it has reached? If anybody thinks he is a prophet or spiritually gifted, let him acknowledge that what I am writing to you is the Lord's command. If he ignores this, he himself will be ignored. Therefore be eager to prophesy and do not forbid speaking in tongues. But everything should be done in a fitting and orderly way.

This passage actually deals with the regulation or control of inspired speech, but because it is often quoted out of context, inconsistencies abound in church practices.

If the words, "Women should remain silent in the Churches. They are not allowed to speak." were taken literally, women would not be able to sing, make an announcement, join in congregational prayer or responsive readings, verbally ask for prayer or teach in the Sunday School. Most people do not interpret it quite so literally - even those who claim to believe in a literal interpretation of other passages. Instead, Paul's words have been used to bar women from varying degrees of involvement in worship, teaching, leading in worship or even serving communion - even though that may not involve any spoken words.

The issue here is more than that of gender roles. It is "an exegetical one that relates to the integrity of Scripture."[49] The central issue is whether the restrictions here contradict the privilege Paul gives to women to pray and prophesy publicly in 1 Corinthians 11. Three options are available and we need to choose what we will believe:

1. It is a misunderstanding that Acts 2:17-18 and 1 Cor. 11:2-16 permit women to prophesy in the church.

2. It is a misunderstanding that 1 Cor. 14:34-35 forbids all vocal, audible participation in the church by women.

3. Paul contradicts himself.

Since 1 Corinthians 11 addresses the "how" of women prophesying, this passage in 1 Corinthians 14 cannot be forbidding them to prophesy for it would be strange indeed for Paul to spend so much time regulating a practice that he planned to forbid further on in his letter.

If Paul permitted speaking in one setting and not in another, there has to be something about either the nature of the speaking or the setting that makes a difference - something that the Corinthian church would have understood but that is not clear to us today.

The first step in sorting through the apparent contradictions is to look at the context of the passage.

What is the context?

Paul is addressing disorder in public worship. Three groups: those speaking in tongues, those prophesying and the talking women were all creating disorder. Paul silenced all three groups (the first two of which must certainly have included men) but he asked for voluntary silence. In order to provide some orderliness to their services, Paul gave three sets of instructions:

1. Only two persons, maybe three, could speak in tongues, but if no interpreter is present the speaker should be silent - sigao (vs. 27-28);

2. Only two or three should prophesy and they were to take turns. If a revelation comes to a second person, the first speaker should stop talking - sigao (vs. 30)

3. Women were to be silent - sigao (vs.34) in the service and to ask their questions at home.

The fact that order was the theme is made clear by the framing of verses 31-33 and 39-40. It is within this frame that Paul addressed the issue of women speaking - no doubt inappropriately interrupting the worship

> *(31-33) For you can all prophesy in turn so that everyone may be instructed and encouraged. (The spirits of the prophets are*

> *subject to the prophets.) For God is not a God of disorder but of peace.*
>
> *(39-40) Therefore be eager to prophesy and do not forbid speaking (laleo) in tongues. But everything should be done in a fitting and orderly way.*

The themes are inclusive participation and order in worship.

What is the meaning of silence?

As Bristow carefully outlines, the word Paul used in this passage is significant.

> The word *phimoo* indicates a forced silence, i.e. when Jesus stilled the raging sea, quieted the unclean spirit, and silenced the Pharisees....Another word, *hesuchia*, is used for silence when the women were to learn in quietness - with a quiet and receptive spirit (1 Tim 2:11-12)....But in this passage, Paul uses *sigao* - a voluntary silence. It is the word used when the disciples decided to remain silent about the transfiguration (Luke 9:3 6) and when Jesus said that if the disciples were silent (*sigao*), the very stones would cry out. It is the word used for Jesus' silence during his trial (Mark 14:61) and the silence of the apostles and elders as they listened to a report by Paul and Barnabas (Acts 15:12). It is a chosen response - or it can also be a request for silence so that someone can speak (Acts 12:17). It is the kind of silence called for in the midst of disorder and tumult.[50]

What is the law to which Paul refers?

Since there is no Old Testament passage that requires female submission, Paul may be using law here as tradition which restricted the public participation of women.[51]

Why could women not speak?

According to Bristow, there are thirty words in Greek which could be translated "speak" - some mean proclaiming, saying, speaking, teaching. But if you wanted to say, "Please do not talk during the prayers," the verb would have to be *laleo*[52] and this is what Paul used. Since Paul's instructions have to do with order in the worship services, it seems perfectly clear that he was telling them not to converse - not to keep on talking during the worship service.

To whom are women to be in submission?

In dealing with 1 Cor. 14:34-35, Atkins makes an interesting observation by asking to whom women are to be subject. The assumption always is that it is to men, but she reveals that the text does not say that; rather, it seems to be to church order since God is not a God of tumult but of peace.[53]

What is Paul really saying?

Paul cannot be saying: "Your women should stop asking questions because women should always be silent," because it would openly contradict the previous regulation of praying and prophesying in the same church. However, he could be saying: "Your women should be silent because they are making too much noise." This is addressing a specific instance where a general principle is being violated: a general principle that people should not disrupt worship services. The specific instance is that the Corinthian women were interrupting the service with their questions.

And Paul can appeal to the example of other churches because this was not happening there. The women in the Corinthian church came from a cultic background known for its noisy religious expressions [and] it seems inconceivable that this background would not have influenced the recent Corinthian converts.[54]

Perhaps here in the Corinthian church, because the women were uneducated, their questions were at such an elementary level that they needed to not interrupt the services but be submissive to the teachers and begin their learning process at home. As their level of learning increased, their questions would then be welcomed.

It seems more appropriate in the context of the whole letter which was about order in worship, that Paul was saying to the women, "Stop talking!" because they were not yet able to ask their questions in a way that was not disruptive.

Paul is not, however, silencing all women for all time. Paul's command in 1 Tim. 2:15 is to "Let the women learn" and questions were a primary method of learning. Here Paul suggests that husbands should take an active role in responding to their wives' lack of biblical education that was characterized by inappropriate questioning.[55]

The teaching in this passage has to do with self-control and appropriate behaviour in worship - avoiding anything that would make the Christian community appear to be like the pagan cults from which the converts had come and thus hinder the spread of the gospel.

Paul is setting forth a principle of order in worship, not the silence of women.

1 Corinthians 15:22

For as in Adam all die, so in Christ all will be made alive

This statement of Paul's is the counter-balance to the 1 Timothy 2:14 text which many use to blame Eve as "the one deceived" for the entrance of sin in the world. Another passage - Romans 5:12 - speaks of sin entering through one man, but uses the Greek word anthropos meaning "human" rather than aner which means "male."

Romans 16:1-16

I commend to you our sister <u>Phoebe</u>, a servant of the church in Cenchrea. I ask you to receive her in the Lord in a way worthy of the saints and to give her any help she may need from you, for she has been a great help to many people, including me. Greet <u>Priscilla</u> and Aquila, my fellow workers in Christ Jesus. They risked their lives for me. Not only I but all the churches of the Gentiles are grateful to them. Greet also the church that meets at their house. Greet my dear friend Epenetus, who was the first convert to Christ in the province of Asia. Greet <u>Mary</u>, who

> *worked very hard for you. Greet Andronicus and <u>Junia</u>, my relatives who have been in prison with me. They are outstanding among the apostles, and they were in Christ before I was. Greet Ampliatus, whom I love in the Lord. Greet Urbanus, our fellow worker in Christ, and my dear friend Stachys. Greet Apelles, tested and approved in Christ. Greet those who belong to the household here, of Aristobulus. Greet Herodion, my relative. Greet those in the household of Narcissus who are in the Lord. Greet <u>Tryphena</u> and <u>Tryphosa</u>, those women who work hard in the Lord. Greet my dear friend <u>Persis,</u> another woman who has worked very hard in the Lord. Greet Rufus, chosen in the Lord, and <u>his mother</u>, who has been a mother to me, too. Greet Asyncritus, Phlegon, Hermes, Patrobas, Hermas and the brothers with them. Greet Philologus, <u>Julia</u>, Nereus and <u>his sister</u>, and Olympas and all the saints with them. Greet one another with a holy kiss. All the churches of Christ send greetings*

This passage clearly shows that Paul lived in harmony with his theory expressed in Galatians 3:28. Here Paul lists various people who have worked for the Lord in various capacities. Of the 28 people, ten of them are women. The term *sun ergos* meaning "co-worker" used here by Paul is the same word he uses in reference to Timothy (1 Th. 3:2) and Titus (2 Cor. 8:23). The term co-worker, as Paul uses it, denotes "a person of the same trade, a colleague."[56] This is ample evidence of the fact that Paul worked alongside women and that the gospel gave women the freedom to exercise their gifts alongside men. One of these women was Phoebe, a *diakonos* of the church. According to Swidler, the early church fathers believed that women could be deacons.

> Clement of Alexandria...clearly refers to women deacons [and] Origen, in commenting on Paul's letter to the Romans and its reference to Phoebe, states: "This text teaches with the authority of the Apostle that even women are instituted deacons in the Church."[57]

Phoebe has also been a *prostatis* of many. Knight claims that the masculine form of this word means "one who stands before, front rank man...leader, chief, but the feminine form, which is used here of Phoebe means "protectress, patroness, helper."[58] Swidler, however, notes that the word appears nowhere else in the New Testament Scripture and always means ruler, leader or protector in all other Greek literature.[59] He also suggests that when Paul uses the verb form of the word in 1 Thessalonians 5:12, it is translated "rule over" and in 1 Timothy 3:4-5 and 5:17 it refers to bishops, priests and deacons.[60] Some churches today prefer the term "ruling elders."

Ephesians 1:10

...to be put into effect when the times will have reached their fulfillment -- to bring all things in heaven and on earth together under one head, even Christ

This use of "head" *(anakephalaioo)* is another example of its use as "source" rather than "boss." Paul speaks of Christ as the final destination of all things. He is the beginning and the end, the Alpha and Omega. This summing up of all things in Christ is described in this text as a recapitulation, or a final recurrence of Christ's headship. In His headship, Christ will contain again within himself all those things of which He was the original source.[61]

(See also 1 Corinthians 11:2-16.)

Ephesians 1:22-23

And God placed all things under his feet and appointed him to be head over everything for the church, which is his body, the fullness of him who fills everything in every way.

The Greek words are *kephale hyper* which means "head above" not *kephale epi* which means "head over." This is a good example of translators bringing their prior understanding of what a word means and superimposing it upon the text when the original words actually say something quite different. If one believes that head means authority, then kephale hyper (head above) can easily be translated "head over." But if the translator approaches Scripture without that prior belief, and attempts to discover the most precise meaning, the concept of "head above" holds other possibilities.

Bilezikian claims that:

> The immediate context of Ephesians 1:22 deals with Christ's superlative transcendence "far above" the opposition, in the remote splendor of the "heavenly places," so that "all things" are below Him, or under His feet. In this exalted position He has no need to establish a relationship of authority over anything. He is above it all. There is only one relationship He maintains in His glorified state, as per divine appointment: He continues to be "head to the church," thus bringing her to completion of her intended "fullness."[62]

Ephesians 4:15-16

Instead, speaking the truth in love, we will in all things grow up into him who is the Head, that is Christ. From him the whole body, joined and held together, by every supporting ligament, grows and builds itself up in love, as each part does its work

When a word has more than one possible meaning, it is always important to look to the context for the definition and in this case the text clearly defines the meaning of *kephale*. The function of the head is to provide "what is necessary for the joining and the knitting together of the body, and He is the source of its growth. The function of the head, according to this passage is to provide life, cohesion and growth."[63]

(See also 1 Corinthians 11:2-16 for more discussion on the use and meaning of *kephale.*)

Ephesians 5:21-33

Submit to one another out of reverence for Christ. Wives, submit to your husbands as to the Lord. For the husband is the head of the wife as Christ is the head of the church, his body, of which he is the Savior. Now as the church submits to Christ, so also wives should submit to their husbands in everything. Husbands, love your wives, just as Christ loved the church and gave himself up for her to make her holy, cleansing her by the washing with water through the word, and to present her to himself as a radiant church, without stain or wrinkle or any other blemish but holy and blameless. In this same way, husbands ought to love their wives as their own bodies. He who loves his wife loves himself. After all, no one ever hated his own body, but he feeds and cares for it, just as Christ does the church--for we are members of his body. "For this reason a man will leave his father and mother and be united to his wife, and the two will become one flesh."(Gen. 2:24) This is a profound mystery--but I am talking about Christ and the church. However, each one of you also must love his wife as he loves himself, and the wife must respect her husband.

The context for these verses is mutual submission - not submission for the wife and dominance for the husband. In the Greek, the verb for submit in verse 21 is not repeated in verse 22. A literal translation would read: "Being subject to one another in the fear of Christ, the wives to their own husbands as to the Lord."

The submission of the wives cannot be separated from mutual submission - one to the other.

Paul continues the idea of mutual submission when he says that, in like manner, the love which a husband is to show his wife is a love which involves the husband's submission - to the point of laying down his life for her as Christ gave himself for the church.

The word 'obey' is not used in regard to wives, whereas it is used for the hierarchical relationship of children and slaves. Not one of the instructions to the husbands refers to ruling. They all entail caring for and building up one's wife.

The main issue in this passage is the meaning of the words "head, submit" and "love."

What is the meaning of Head?

Bilezikian indicates that in this passage, Paul explains the meaning of the word "head" when he adds the explanation that Christ is himself the Saviour of the Body. He says that:

the emphatic pronoun rendered here "himself" indicates that Paul makes a point of the fact that saviorhood pertains to Christ's headship. This servant-ministry of the Savior receives further elaboration in verse 25: "Christ loved the church and gave himself up for her," and in verse 29: "for no man ever hates his own flesh, but nourishes it and cherishes it, as Christ does the church." The motif of Christ as the source of nurture appears again in this passage.[64]

(See also 1 Corinthians 11:2-16.)

What is the meaning of Submission?

Atkins defines submission by saying it is NOT silence, financial or emotional dependence, domesticity, or manipulation, but rather it is "to put aside any devices one might use for one's own profit, and to put one's entire life at someone else's disposal."[65]

Bilezikian argues that although the usual meaning of submit is "to make oneself subordinate to the authority of a higher power, to be dependent for direction on the desires of a superior in rank, or position, [or] to yield to rulership,"[66] the meaning is changed entirely in this text. "Being subject to one another" is a very different relationship from "being subject to the other."[67] He goes on to say that:

> being subject to one another is only possible among equals. It is a mutual (two-way) process that excludes the unilateral (one-way) subordination implicit in the concept of subjection without the reciprocal pronoun. Mutual subjection suggests horizontal lines of interaction among equals [rather than] top-down dominance of ruler over subject.[68]

There were several words Paul could have used if the idea he wanted to convey was obedience. Paul uses the Greek word *hupakouo* (Eph.6:5) in reference to slaves, and *peitharcheo* (Eph.6:1) when he speaks of children.[69] Bristow points out that the fact that Paul did not use either of these words shows that, unlike the Greek philosophers who would place wives, along with children and slaves under the authority of men, Paul had no intention of doing so.

Another word *hupotasso* was available for him to use, which in the active form means "to subordinate." Paul uses it

> only to tell what God does, but he does not tell husbands to *hupotasso* their wives. Instead, by using the middle voice form *hupotassomai* he is appealing to wives to voluntarily be subject to their husbands. Since it is asking for something that is voluntary by nature, *hupotassomai* means something like "give allegiance to", "tend to the needs of" "be supportive of" or "be responsive to." In the same way, Paul appealed to the members of the church to *hupotassomai* one another. This is not a ranking of persons as ruler and ruled, but a concise appeal for the Church to have its members live out their call to be "the body of Christ." What is true of the Church, Paul added, is to be true of a marriage.[70]

What is the meaning of Love?

The third significant word which Bristow examines is *agapao*, which Paul uses in his instruction to husbands to "love" their wives. This word is almost identical with *hupotassomai*. Both involve giving up one's self-interest to serve and care for the needs of the other. And both are commended to all Christians, as well as to husbands and wives. Bristow elaborates on the fact that in Jewish literature, a favorite form of writing involved using synonyms in parallel fashion: Wives are to *hupotassomai* their husbands; husbands are to *agapao* their wives.[71] He goes on to point out that this created a new model for Christian marriage. A husband is not to boss his wife but is to "nourish and sanctify his wife and even be willing to die for her."[72]

"In a culture where husbands had little regard for the feelings and needs of their wives, and where wives had little knowledge of the concerns of their husbands, Paul's advice to husbands and wives must have shocked his hearers."[73]

Colossians 3:18-25

<u>Wives</u>, submit to your husbands as is fitting in the Lord. <u>Husbands</u>, love your wives and do not be harsh with them. <u>Children</u>, obey your parents in everything, for this pleases the Lord.

...and do it, not only when their eye is on you and to win their favor, but with sincerity of heart and reverence for the Lord. Whatever you do, work at it with your heart, as working for the Lord, not for men, since you know that you will receive an inheritance from the Lord as a reward. It is the Lord Christ you are serving. Anyone who does wrong will be repaid for his wrong, and there is no favoritism.

This is one of the passages in which "household codes" are spelled out. It is clear that Paul says women are to submit to their husbands, but it is also clear that he does not command them to obey as he does children and slaves. The key is to understand the meaning of submission and to see this in light of the whole of Scripture, in which he requires mutual submission. Also, as Craig Keener points out in *Paul, Women and Wives*, Paul is writing to a culture where men usually led in the homes and "if Paul could call on slaves to submit without supporting slavery, we must allow that he could have asked wives to submit without supporting male dominance."[74]

1 Timothy 2:8-15

I want men everywhere to lift up holy hands in prayer, without anger or disputing. I also want women to dress modestly, with decency and propriety, not with braided hair or gold or pearls or expensive clothes, but with good deeds, appropriate for women who profess to worship God. A woman should learn in quietness and full submission. I do not permit a woman to teach or to have authority over a man; she must be silent. For Adam was formed first, then Eve. And Adam was not the one deceived; it was the woman who was deceived and became a sinner. But women will be saved through childbearing--if they continue in faith, love and holiness with propriety.

This is the passage those who believe in the subordination of women have used to silence any woman who would fill a position that might be perceived as "exercising authority" over a man. In the same way that the specific teaching about women in 1 Corinthians 14 needs to be looked at in its context, rather than taken in isolation, so we must be careful to discover the context for this passage. The purpose of this letter was to give practical advice to Timothy regarding the people who were responsible for false teaching in his congregation. Timothy was to protect the church from heresy by silencing those teaching false doctrines, myths and endless genealogies (verse 3).

Those who maintain a hierarchical stance claim that Paul is making a flat prohibition of any woman anywhere doing any teaching or exercising any authority over any man. But when read in context, in Greek, with careful study of the words, it is not as clear as some would think.

Let's look first at what is clear.

It is clear what women ARE to do: Learn

The main point in this passage is that women should be taught. The only commandment here is, "Let a woman learn" and the appeal to creation is that Eve was deceived. Deception is an "inevitable result of ignorance...[and] the solution is obvious. Let women learn and they will not be so easily deceived."[75]

Knight says that Paul's reference to Eve being beguiled is related to the roles being reversed, but in fact, the reference to being deceived relates to the context of this whole passage. The COMMAND (not "request" as Knight suggests) is that women should learn. "Let the women learn" is the imperative in this sentence! The message is that women need to learn because lack of learning leads to deception. Anyone who has not been taught can be deceived and anyone who is easily deceived certainly should not teach.

In spite of the fact that "[p]roviding education for women...ran the risk of moral censure from non-Christians...[because teachers] at first had to be only men, for only men were educated in the faith and Jewish custom strictly forbade women from conversing with men other than their husbands,"[76] Paul mandated that the women should be taught. Bristow asserts that:

> Paul's desire that women be educated in the faith was both radical in thought and difficult in execution....Women were not used to listening to lectures or thinking about theological concepts, or studying at all. Therefore, Paul instructed them to learn, but "in silence and subjection" (1 Tim. 2:11). The word for subjection is *hupotassomai* which is the voluntary willingness to be responsive to the needs of others. Just as in worship (1 Cor. 14) so in study: women are to be considerate of others. But the word for silence is *hesuchia*. It does not mean simply refraining from talking. It means restful quietness, as in meditation and study. A few sentences before, Paul used this same word to describe the peaceful and quiet life that he wished for all believers.[77]

In the context, then, of countering false doctrines, Paul's command to the church is for the women to learn, and the expression "in silence" is the manner in which they ought to learn. The injunction against teaching is obviously because the women needed to learn first.[78]

It is clear what women are NOT to do: Authentein

Another issue in this Timothy passage is the use of the word *authentein* which has been translated "have authority." There is no consensus on the meaning of *authentein* but one thing is certain: that if Paul had intended to restrict women from having authority in the normal sense of the word, it is reasonable to assume that he would have used the normal word, *exousia*. Paul, by using a singularly different word - a word used nowhere else in the New Testament, indicates that he is talking about something quite different here. The historian Josephus uses [*authentein*] to describe Antipas, Herod's son, accused of killing his two brothers and attempting to kill his father....Thus *authentein* signifies 'to domineer' or 'to have absolute power over' persons in such a way as to destroy them.[79]

Bristow says that *authenteo* is opposite to the spirit of love and respect that Paul commended to all Christians.[80]

It is important to note that Paul's refusal to allow women to domineer over men does not in any way give permission for men to domineer over women. Leadership which overpowers and destroys is never sanctioned by Christ for either men or women.

What is not clear is Paul's reason for the prohibition.

Some traditionalists say that Paul's refusal to allow women to teach is not cultural but is based on the creation order and is therefore still binding on us today. Knight says that:

> That which is prohibited is teaching (*didaskein*) and having dominion (*authentein*). The prohibition is not that a woman may not teach anyone, but that within the church she must not teach and have authority over a man (*andros*).'[81]

He goes on to say that the "reason for such a vigorous prohibition follows immediately in verses 13 and 14: "For it was Adam who was first created, and then Eve."[82]

Knight makes several assumptions about creation, which, taken as fact, become the foundation for his beliefs. One is that "the order in which God created man and woman expresses and determines the relationship God intended and the order of authority. The one formed first is to have dominion, the one formed after and from him is to be in subjection."[83] That is an interpretation brought to the text rather than found in the text. Knight's prior belief system that men are dominant, and women subordinate, clearly influences his interpretation of Scripture. His framework, rather than being the creation story, is in fact the "Fall" which he makes normative. There is nothing in the Genesis account of creation indicating that dominion and subjection are related to the order of creation (see section III A). Any subjection or "ruling" comes as a result of sin and therefore cannot be read into God's intended creation order.

It is possible that Paul, instead of being concerned with hierarchy in this passage, is countering Gnostic teaching. Some Gnostics taught that the first man was androgynous until cut in two with Adam and Eve then becoming separate individuals; others taught that Eve gave birth to Adam[84] (another possible meaning of *authetein* is "the originator" or "author" of). Paul corrects this teaching by declaring that Adam was formed first, and then Eve.

Another Gnostic teaching was that Adam was ignorant while Eve was informed of the truth, but Paul counters that teaching by saying that while Eve was utterly deceived, Adam was not deceived. For anyone to take this [text] to mean that Paul is arguing for the leadership of men on the basis of these facts is absurd. As Catherine Kroeger declares, "Such an argument would be saying that a willful sinner is better than a deceived sinner. This would give us a church in which knaves governed fools."[85]

Other Gnostics would lay no blame on Eve, saying that she was "informed of the truth [through] the fruit of the tree of Knowledge (Gnosis)."[86] In this passage, although he elsewhere lays the responsibility for sin entering the world on Adam (1 Cor. 15:21), Paul declares that Eve could not have been the one who brought truth because Eve became "in transgression" (that is, violating the law of God).[87]

Paul then makes the difficult statement, "But she will be saved through child-bearing." There are various possible interpretations of this, none of which are completely clear.

What it can't mean is that women are saved by bearing children. That idea is contrary to all the rest of Scripture and those who say Scripture means what it says in verse 12 (I do not permit a woman to teach or have authority over a man) will agree that it can't mean what it says when they get to verse 15 (women will be saved through childbearing).

One possible meaning is that the childbearing refers to the specific birth of the Christ child, so that Paul could be saying, as Bristow suggests:

> You who regard women as spiritually inferior because of the example of Eve, remember that when God provided a means of salvation for us all, he did so through the cooperation of a woman, Mary. And you Gnostics who regard the physical as evil, my gospel tells me that my Redeemer was born of a woman,

flesh and blood born of flesh and blood, and that by this means the good news of salvation is offered to all who have faith and love and sanctification.[88]

Another possibility is that this is a correction to a heresy which did not value women who were married and mothers. In some cults there was a tendency to downplay marriage and elevate those who remained celibate. Paul wanted wives and mothers to know that they were under blessing, not under a curse. Spirituality does not require celibacy.

A third possible interpretation put forth by Catherine and Richard Kroeger in *I Suffer Not a Woman* relates to the Gnostic teaching that women had to become men in order to be saved. Paul counters that by declaring that women will be saved as women (the child-bearers) in the same way that men are: by continuing in faith, love and holiness.

A fourth suggested interpretation is that a woman will be protected in childbirth. And still another is that childbearing is a metaphor for the fulfillment of the calling God places on a woman.

Certainly, what is evident is that the meaning of this verse is open to speculation, although we can be certain that those who understood the context would not have been confused.

Summary

In the context of false teaching which must be silenced, Paul is admonishing the women to submit themselves to the teaching of sound doctrine.

Seen in the context of the whole letter, it is clear that this passage does not intend to eliminate women from the role of ministry in the church. When people make this verse the keystone which controls all other verses, they are attempting to legitimize a previously decided upon position. This kind of interpretive practice does not do justice to the whole of Scripture.

Paul wrote this letter to Timothy to help him deal with the influence of the pagan converts who were corrupting Christian truth with

Gnostic thinking. All the messages about women fit into the category of either refuting Gnostic teaching or dealing with appropriate behaviour for Christians living in a pagan culture. The teaching of this passage makes sense when understood, not as a statement of hierarchy, but as a countering of a series of heretical Gnostic teachings.

Gnostic teaching: Eve was not deceived but brought truth.

> Paul counters: "No, it was Eve who was deceived; she could not be the source of truth."

Gnostic teaching: Eve gave birth to Adam - she was the originator.

> Paul counters: "No, I do not permit women to teach that they are the originator (author) of men. Adam was created *first*, then Eve."

Gnostic teaching: Women had to become men in order to be saved.

> Paul counters: "No, women will be saved as woman, (the ones who bear children) - in the same way as men - through faith, love and holiness."

Paul's reference to Eve being deceived was intended as a warning to the whole church - not just to the women. It is not consistent with the rest of Pauline theology to insist that because Eve was deceived, women forever will be deceived and therefore cannot be trusted to teach. Adam's sin of disobedience does not mean that males are forever disobedient and therefore unable to follow through on God's commissioning. Paul insists that the blood of Christ cleanses us from all unrighteousness. Why then, would Eve's deception not also be redeemed by the blood of Christ?

1 Timothy 3:1-13

> *If anyone sets his heart on being an overseer, he desires a noble task. Now the overseer must be above reproach, the husband of but one wife, temperate, self- controlled, respectable, hospitable, able to teach, not given to drunkenness, not violent but gentle, not quarrelsome, not a lover of money. He must manage his own family well and see that his children obey him with proper respect. (If anyone does not know how to manage his own family, how can he take care of God's church?) He must not be a recent convert, or he may become conceited and fall under*

> *the same judgment as the devil. He must also have a good reputation with outsiders, so that he will not fall into disgrace and into the devil's trap. Deacons, likewise, are to be men worthy of respect, sincere, not indulging in much wine, and not pursuing dishonest gain. They must keep hold of the deep truths of the faith with a clear conscience. They must first be tested; and then if there is nothing against them, let them serve as deacons. In the same way, <u>their wives</u> are to be women worthy of respect, not malicious talkers but temperate and trustworthy in everything. A deacon must be the husband of but one wife and must manage his children and his household well. Those who have served well gain an excellent standing and great assurance in their faith in Christ Jesus.*

This letter of Paul to Timothy is often used to exclude women from the role of a spiritual leader because the passage requires an overseer to be the husband of one wife. The intent does not appear to be the exclusion of women, but rather to stress the importance of monogamy for spiritual leadership. Obviously the spiritual leaders would normally have been men because they would have the education and the cultural role. It is the men who are addressed in this regard because only men would have had more than one wife. A woman was not permitted to have more than one husband. In addition to that, Paul specifically avoids excluding women by using the inclusive "anyone" (If "anyone" desires the office of bishop) and although the English translations frequently use the word "man," it is not in the Greek text. As well, "their wives" (see underlined text) may be translated "women" referring to female deacons as Phoebe was (Romans 16:1-3). This means women were addressed "in the same way" as men.

1 Timothy 5:1-2

> *Do not rebuke an older man harshly, but exhort him as if he were your father. Treat younger men as brothers, older women as mothers, and younger women as sisters, with absolute purity.*

Paul was here continuing to give Timothy practical instructions - this time about his relationships with a variety of people. He uses the same term for older women *(presbytera)* as he does for older men *(presbyteros)* which is the term for ruling elders (1 Tim. 5:17*)*.

Titus 1:5-16

The reason I left you in Crete was that you might straighten out what was left unfinished and appoint elders in every town, as I directed you. An elder must be blameless, the husband of but one wife, a man whose children believe and are not open to the charge of being wild and disobedient. Since an overseer is entrusted with God's work, he must be blameless--not overbearing, not quick-tempered, not given to drunkenness, not violent, not pursuing dishonest gain. Rather he must be hospitable, one who loves what is good, who is self-controlled, upright, holy and disciplined. He must hold firmly to the trustworthy message as it has been taught, so that he can encourage others by sound doctrine and refute those who oppose it. For there are many rebellious people, mere talkers and deceivers, especially those of the circumcision group.

They must be silenced, because they are ruining whole households by teaching things they ought not to teach--and that for the sake of dishonest gain. Even one of their own prophets has said, "Cretans are always liars, evil brutes, lazy gluttons." This testimony is true. Therefore, rebuke them sharply, so that they will be sound in the faith and will pay no attention to Jewish myths or to the commands of those who reject the truth. To the pure, all things are pure, but to those who are corrupted and do not believe, nothing is pure. In fact, both their minds and consciences are corrupted. They claim to know God, but by their actions they deny him. They are detestable, disobedient and unfit for doing anything good.

The people who were to be silenced here must certainly have included men since most of the teaching would have been carried out by men. This lends credence to the idea that silence was not for all time, but was directed to certain groups of people in certain situations. Paul's concern for the teaching of truth required that he speak strongly and clearly to any situation which would allow for the distortion of the truth that he had taught them.

Titus 2:1-10

> *You must teach what is in accord with sound doctrine. Teach the older men to be temperate, worthy of respect, self-controlled, and sound in faith, in love and in endurance. Likewise, teach the older women to be reverent in the way they live, not to be slanderers or addicted to much wine, but to teach what is good. Then they can train the younger women to love their husbands and children, to be self-controlled and pure, to be busy at home, to be kind, and to be subject to their husbands, so that no one will malign the word of God. Similarly, encourage the young men to be self-controlled. In everything set them an example by doing what is good. In your teaching show integrity, seriousness and soundness of speech that cannot be condemned, so that those who oppose you may be ashamed because they have nothing bad to say about us. Teach slaves to be subject to their masters in everything, to try to please them, not to talk back to them, and not to steal from them, but to show that they can be fully trusted, so that in every way they will make the teaching about God our Savior attractive.*

The message in this passage is that what is taught about Christian behaviour is to be in accordance with the teaching of sound doctrine. Belief and behaviour are to match. Non-believers watch the behaviour of Christians and if it matches what they say, the Word of God is honoured, but if it does not, the Word of God is maligned. The specifics of how this was to be worked out was a cultural issue for women just as it was for slaves. Paul was not suggesting that slavery as an institution was God-ordained when he required slaves to live in a way that revealed Christian character. Nor was he setting out a principle that women were to stay at home and only teach younger women when he instructed them to live within the expectations of their culture in a way that revealed their Christian character. They were to model a life that was consistent with their life in Christ within the societal norms of the time.

6. The Church's Demonstration of the New Model

Not only did Paul make statements that were often shocking, but his practice of having men and women together in worship must have raised many questions for his Jewish and pagan contemporaries.

The apostles early began to speak of the "women of our company" (Luke 24:22). When the apostles were engaged in prayer, they did so "together with the women" (Acts 1:14). After the day of Pentecost, "multitudes, both men and women" were welcomed into the fellowship of believers (Acts 5:14) and both men and women were baptized (Acts 8:12).[89]

The importance of the place of women in the Church is further indicated by the fact that Saul arrested both men and women believers (Acts 8:3, Acts 9:1-2 and Acts 22:4-5).

The same disregard for social restrictions of contact between men and women and the same abandoning of any protectionistic attitudes regarding women that characterized Paul's passion when he persecuted the Church continued to characterize Paul's passion when he became an apostle of the Church.[90]

The strongest argument in support of women participating fully in the church comes from Peter's quoting of Joel 2:28-32 on the Day of Pentecost. As Bristow points out:

> It would be strange indeed if the church, under the apostles, regarded this as a sign of the new age in Christ and yet forbade women the right to give inspired messages to the Church![91]

Not only was Peter's sermon recorded, but the epistle of Peter indicates the degree to which the early Christians were being taught to live out the new relationship between men and women.

1 Peter 3:1-8

Wives, in the same way be submissive to your husbands so that, if any of them do not believe the word, they may be won over without words by the behavior of their wives, when they see the

> *purity and reverence of your lives. Your beauty should not come from outward adornment, such as braided hair and the wearing of gold jewelry and fine clothes. Instead, it should be that of your inner self, the unfading beauty of a gentle and quiet spirit, which is of great worth in God's sight. For this is the way the holy women of the past who put their hope in God used to make themselves beautiful. They were submissive to their own husbands, like Sarah, who obeyed Abraham and called him her master. You are her daughters if you do what is right and do not give way to fear.*
>
> *Husbands, in the same way be considerate as you live with your wives and treat them with respect as the weaker partner and as heirs with you of the gracious gift of life so that nothing will hinder your prayers. Finally, all of you, live in harmony with one another; be sympathetic, as brothers, be compassionate and humble.*

The context of this passage is the Christian way of relating: mutual submission, mutual service and mutual love. And the specific context is winning the unsaved to Christ.

The reference to Sarah obeying Abraham reminds us of her ability and willingness to trust God and not "give way to fear" even in the face of Abraham's age and his cowardice. (He pretended she was his sister, putting her at risk, in order to protect his own life.) Here, Peter is telling women whose husbands have not become Christians that they would be Sarah's daughters if they follow her example and do not "submit out of fear...[but] place their confidence in God."[92] The consequence may well be that their husbands will be won over by the beauty and reverence of their wives.

The verses preceding this passage deal with slaves who are to submit to their masters, and the transition from slaves to wives is made with the important word translated "in the same manner." The servant attitude modeled by Christ and required of slaves is also the example for wives.[93]

Peter then addressed Christian men and said that if they fail to give their wives the respect due them, their prayers would be hindered.

And the surprising thing is that the transition from wives to husbands is made using exactly the same words: "in the same way." The servant attitude modeled by Christ and required of slaves and wives is also the example for husbands. As Bilezikian argues,

> the apostle Peter subjects husbands to a traumatic role reversal. Under the patriarchal system, it was the duty of wives "to live considerately" with their husbands, "bestowing honor" on [them]...to regard husbands as the supreme heirs to the blessings of life....Now it is husbands who must show consideration for their wives and bestow honor upon them, much as a servant to his master. Women...in the new creation...become "joint heirs with their husbands." Both husband and wife have become equal recipients of the grace that is the source of their new life. And should husbands default in any of those areas by reverting to carnal self-assertive ways, they might as well cease praying. By acting like masters to their wives instead of servants, they create a spiritual obstruction that makes them and therefore their prayers unacceptable to God.[94]

Martin describes how the early Christians "testified against infanticide, polygamy, and divorce and began to apply the principle of sexual fidelity to both marriage partners"[95] indicating the positive effect that Christian principles had on the condition of women. Thus, the early church began to live out the message of the gospel in all its fullness which for women was a message of unprecedented freedom.

Discussion and Reflection Questions

1. Describe a situation in which you have seen those in authority "lord it over" others?

2. It is difficult to see the events described in Scripture through the perspective of the original participants, but try to put yourself in the Jewish culture of Jesus' day and then describe which encounter between Jesus and a woman you think would have been the most shocking in that culture? Why would it have been shocking? What do you think the reaction of the woman involved might have been? What do you think the reaction of the women watching from the sidelines might have been? Can you think of a similar situation in today's culture?

3. As a result of the actions and words of Jesus in these passages, what would you say are the determining factors for Christian ministry?

4. How would you answer the question, "Does the order of redemption impact all of life here and now or only the spiritual reality?"

5. How does Paul's admonition to the three groups of people in 1 Corinthians 14 benefit the community of believers?

6. What would a church look like if its members were to say, "I submit myself" *(hupotassomai)* to one another?

7. Would Paul's clear direction that sexual relations within marriage are to be by mutual consent have been a radical statement when he wrote it? Is it today?

8. If the "one flesh" union mandates mutuality on decision making, would that apply to decisions within congregations which exist as the "one body" of Christ?

9. When the framework of redemption is used consistently, how does that affect the practical working out of passages such as Galatians 3:28, Ephesians 5:21-33, or 1 Timothy 1:1-13?

10. Summarize the teaching in the various passages on the use of *kephale* (head) in Paul's writings.

11. 1 Timothy 2:15 is a difficult passage. What have you been taught that it says? What are other options for interpreting it? Which of them seems most consistent with the rest of Scripture?

12. Can you imagine what the message of the gospel must have meant to the women in Jesus' life? The women in Paul's life? What about today?

13. What challenge is there for you personally in Paul's letter to Titus regarding living a life that is consistent with the doctrine taught in Scripture? Would you need to make any changes? If so, what impact would that have on your Christian community of brothers and sisters in Christ? On the non-Christians watching you?

14. What principles for communal worship would you draw from 1Corinthians 14:26-35?

Chapter 4
IDENTIFYING THE CULTURAL INFLUENCES

The challenge here is to acknowledge the influences that mold our theology

A. Acknowledging Personal Beliefs

There is no such thing as a totally objective reading of Scripture because we all bring prior beliefs to the text. Our personal agenda and our deeply held beliefs are always present; however, greater objectivity can be achieved when we are made aware of the influences that have helped to form our beliefs. A brief overview of some historical teachings will shed some light on the influences that have determined the interpretation of passages concerning women. It is important to understand our own biases as well as those of others who influence our interpretation and therefore our belief system.

>No one has NO bias.

>No one is immune to pride.

>No one is immune to self-deceit.

B. Shaping of Beliefs

The original Scripture texts have not changed since they were written but our interpretations have certainly changed. The framework we use as individuals is a major factor in how we understand Scripture but, as well, the traditional messages we have been taught have an impact on the way Scripture is understood. A brief overview of the role of women in Judaism and in the church will reveal the way these influences have shaped our understanding of the role of women.

1. View of Women in Judaism

Although women held significant leadership roles in the Jewish world of the Old Testament, the predominant attitude toward women was negative. Swidler in *Biblical Affirmations of Women* details the rabbinic teachings about women (see Chapter 3 section B1 for details).

Swidler documents that women were not permitted to participate in public prayer, not counted in a quorum, classified with children and slaves, limited to the Gentiles' court and the women's court in the temple, not to be greeted by a male in the street, not allowed to bear witness in a court, and they lived with the teaching of the Rabbis that death in childbirth was punishment for causing the death of Adam.[1]

2. View of Women in the Early Church

As Spencer points out, the rending of the curtain at the time of Jesus' crucifixion dramatically changed the role of women.

> The torn curtain signifies that now God's Spirit no longer dwells in a place but in a people. The people of God have become a movable tent, the sanctuary of God. And as the Spirit moves out from the Holy of Holies, the barrier between the Holy Place is swung back. Then God moves out from the Holy Place to the Court of the Priests, eliminating the specially chosen priest. Then the barrier between priest and layperson is eradicated as God moves to the Court of the Israelites. The barrier between man and woman is

removed as God moves to the Court of Women. At last, the final gate collapses when the Court of the Gentiles is reached. The movement outward that the Spirit made from the innermost sanctuary to the peripheral courts in the temple signifies the priority Jesus had on earth in dealing with different groups.[2]

The church, in its infancy, made great advances in the freedom given to women to participate in ministry in response to their call by God. (For a detailed study see Chapter 3 section B The New Paradigm of Redemption.)

3. View of Women in the First Few Centuries

History is commonly defined as:

> systematic narration and critical interpretation of events worthy of memory in human society....The writing of history, then, has not been...[an] objective exercise; the events it brings to light are rather the result of choices made by the historian to bring out what his personal, social and political outlook considers interesting and 'worthy' of being remembered.[3]

When we then look to the early church fathers (notably Tertullian, Augustine, Ambrose, Epiphanius and Aquinas) for direction regarding an understanding of the role of women, we must recognize that their recording of history has been influenced by their own paradigm.

The early church fathers rarely gave women authority because they genuinely believed that they were spiritually inferior.[4] They truly doubted that women were made in the image of God. Although this belief still prevails in the minds of some, opponents made no such distinction, for women were martyred along with men. In AD 203, Perpetua, at the age of 21, was martyred in Carthage, North Africa. She kept a diary when she was in prison and it is the first known writing of any woman in Latin prose. Her life and writings inspired later preachers but they attributed her faithfulness in the face of death to her "manly" traits.[5]

Tertullian (AD 160-225) taught that woman was a beguiling temptress, that daughters of Eve should wear penitential garb and he blamed women for the suffering of mankind. He said:

> Do you not know that you are [each] an Eve? The sentence of God - on this sex of yours - lives in this age; the guilt must necessarily live, too....You are the devil's gateway; you are the unsealer of that [forbidden] tree; you are the first deserter of the divine law.[6]

Epiphanius (AD 315-403) said, "the female sex is easily seduced, weak, and without much understanding"....Ambrose (AD 339-397) taught that when women believed, their female character faded and they took on the virtues of the male sex....Augustine (AD 354-430) preached sermons about Perpetua saying that the manliness of her soul hides the sex of her flesh. He also said that, "woman represented the physical while man represented the spiritual."[7]

Augustine allowed woman a slight advantage if she were married:

> The woman together with her husband is the image of God, so that the whole substance is one image, but when she is assigned as a help-mate, a function that pertains to her alone, then she is not the image of God, but, as far as the man is concerned, he is by himself alone the image of God, just as fully and completely as when he and the woman are joined together into one.[8]

In the year 584, in Lyon, France, 63 Bishops and representatives voted 32 to 31 in favour of the question, "Are women human?" Women were declared human by one vote.[9]

One voice among those negative ones who spoke out for women was Clement of Alexandria, a contemporary of Tertullian's and head of the Christian school in that city until driven out by persecution in AD 203. He insisted that men and women alike may "philosophize."[10]

Bristow asserts that it was the writings of the early church fathers, especially Augustine, which significantly influenced the thinking of the generations to follow and because they were influenced by the Greek philosophical framework in which they been educated, male leaders were "given a sexual bias that naturally led them to interpret Paul's writings in a like manner of thought." Eventually,

> the model that gained favor in the church was not the one voiced by Paul, [but by Aristotle], a pagan philosopher five centuries older, defended in the sanctuaries and cathedrals of the Christian faith by quoting the words of Paul, as translated, out of context, without reference to that ideal close to Paul's heart that he so earnestly sought for the church, that there be sexual equality among Christians.[11]

Thus the model presented by Paul, which began to get lived out in the early church, was systematically destroyed by the philosophies of the surrounding cultures. And then Paul's ideal of sexual equality within the Church was dealt a mortal blow:

> Constantine gave his favor to the faith of the Christians. Christianity became fashionable...and those who would court imperial favor began to join the Church....Many cared [little] about the teachings of Christ. As the Church became more and more transformed by the world, its life took on more of the characteristics of Hellenized Roman society....Slowly the teachings of Greek philosophy interbred with Christian theology, producing a brood of beliefs that were often pagan in their assumptions.[12]

This pagan view of women influenced Christianity through Roman civilization, until, "[the] very backbone of the church, her canon law, institutionalized the place of women - under the authority of men."[13]

4. View of Women in the Middle Ages

The defeat of Paul's ideal of sexual equality culminated in the writings of Thomas Aquinas (1225-1274) who agreed with Aristotle that woman "is defective and misbegotten."[14] By then, the deprecation of womanhood was completely fused into Christian theology, based on Aquinas' interpretation of the words of the apostle Paul.[15]

Saint Bonaventure (1217-1274) denounced women by agreeing with Aristotle's scathing comments[16] and Duns Scotus (1226-1308) "concluded that although there would be benefits in ordaining women, those benefits could not be considered because Christ had willed otherwise."[17]

Martin points out that two contradictory teachings about women were accepted in the Middle Ages:

> Women were simultaneously despised as daughters of Eve, the temptress, and adored in the tradition of the Virgin Mary....Writers, who would have been mostly monks, extolled either Eve or Mary as the true paradigm of the feminine gender, each claiming in doing so, to understand the true female nature.[18]

5. View of Women in the Modern Period

Martin Luther (1483-1546) declared, "Women should remain at home, sit still, keep house, and bear and bring up children....If a woman grows weary and, at last, dies from childbearing, it matters not. Let her die from childbearing - she is there to do it."[19] He claims that, although she is a very excellent work of God, [woman] was created "inferior to men in both honor and dignity."[20] He did, however, open up the possibility of a public ministry for women in situations where no men were available, in which case "it might be necessary for the women to preach."[21]

Charles Hodge (1797-1878) saw woman as equal to man with respect to "knowledge, righteousness and holiness" but not with regard to

"God's authority." She is not designed to reflect the glory of God as ruler, but is, in this respect, subordinate to the man.[22]

A giant step toward equality was taken when John Calvin (1509-1564) declared that woman was in fact created in the image of God, even though it was in "the second degree."[23]

The Reformation, with its negative view of convents, offered women only the traditional role of wife and mother...and lay ministries were severely curtailed.[24] This meant that, while "men were offered an opportunity to have meaningful full-time ministries," [25] a single woman "lacked the only relationship that could give spiritual meaning to her life: marriage."[26]

During the early to mid 1800's, women were leaders as both revivalists and abolitionists. They began to advocate greater opportunities and rights for women in church and society including women's preaching. Charles Finney (1792-1874) created an uproar by permitting women to pray and testify in public meetings, maintaining that "the church that silences women is shorn of half its power."[27]

6. Role of Women Today

As Martin observes, "To be denied the image of God is to be eliminated from God's revealed purpose for human life."[28] Today, although the heresy that women are not image bearers of God has been abandoned, their role in the church has not changed significantly. Martin observes that:

> Woman has at last been given the theological position of spiritual equality with man [but] she is not to have practical equality....In God's eyes you are equal, but in men's eyes you must be unequal.[29]

Not only has the role of women not changed significantly in many churches, but there is often a concerted effort to make sure that women are kept subordinate. Bilezikian claims that some will even resort to heresy about the nature of God in order to find support for their preconceived argument that man must have authority over woman. The following information is taken from notes of his lecture, "Subordination in the Godhead: A Re-Emerging Heresy:"[30]

> The writings of the early Church Fathers reveal the struggle to establish the doctrine of the Trinity against the false teaching of subordinationism which asserts that there is an eternal hierarchy within the Godhead.
>
> This heresy was clearly denounced when an ecumenical council of bishops met in AD 325. They developed the Nicean Creed which affirms the full divinity of Christ - the essential oneness of the Trinity. Father, Son and Holy Spirit share the same essence. This settled the relationship of the Trinity and made historical gains in the controversy about the divine and human nature of Jesus. The creed established that Jesus humbled himself (that no one subordinated him) and that his self-humiliation was temporary, not eternal (that it was related to his ministry, not his being). The council denied there was any hierarchy within the Godhead and rejected subordinationism as pagan infiltration.
>
> However, Arius of Alexandria openly opposed the bishops and taught that only the Father was eternal. The Son was a created being and therefore there was a time when the Son was not. He denied that the Son had equality with God, saying that they were different in essence.
>
> Subordinationism, although dealt with by the early church, continues to emerge from time to time and is the basis upon which the Watchtower Society (Jehovah's Witnesses) is founded. Its re-emergence today in relation to the role of woman is significant because it serves to substantiate hierarchy in the very nature of God, not just in God's created world.

> Belief that an eternal relationship of authority and obedience exists between the Father and Son, results in the belief that there is also a relationship of authority and obedience between men and women because humans are created in the image of God. Hierarchy is then grounded in the being of God. In order to achieve Godlikeness among humans, the relation of authority and submission must be exercised not only in marriage and the church, but it must also be extended to the rest of human activity - to the whole of life.
>
> This belief contends that, not only are women to be obedient to men in all areas of life on earth but also in the life to come, because man images God throughout eternity.

In contrast to this unbiblical position, Martin strongly maintains that "male authority is not a doctrine of authentic Christianity; it originated under the influence of society."[31] She claims that a patronizing attitude toward women is at the heart of the conservative argument for the submission of women.

In his response to those who hold to male hierarchy, W. Ward Gasque writes that "the evidence of Scripture is not so clear as those who take the traditionalist position on the role of women seem to assume."[32] He goes on to say that we have different roles and functions in the world, but to "use Scripture to keep women...subservient to men is...a most perverse handling of the word of God."[33]

C. Challenging Biases

The statement made at the beginning of this section: "no one has NO bias," might indicate that we cannot hope to see truth. Fortunately our biases can be challenged.

Most of us have grown up hearing stories of women in the Bible. The biases of the storytellers and the translators have influenced the way those stories have been handed down to us, and have in turn created our understanding of the role of women. This is how biases are perpetuated as truth. For example:

- Eve is blamed for Man's fall, but scripture clearly says that sin entered by one man.
- Bathsheba is blamed for David's sin, but God through Nathan held David accountable.
- Eve is seen as "helper" meaning servant, but *'ezer* usually refers to God in the Old Testament.
- Phoebe is called a servant when the Greek word is "deacon."

The way to challenge biases is to begin to ask questions, to try to read a story from another perspective, to allow for the possibility that our assumptions may be based on someone else's bias rather than on the truth.

Questions that need to be addressed today include: What is the role of tradition? What concessions have been made to culture in the past? What concessions are we making today to culture? Does the culture inform the church or the church inform culture?

Throughout history, circumstances have changed the idea of what lifestyle a Christian will live in order to reveal their spirituality. In the early church, when Christians were martyred for their faith, martyrdom was seen as the ultimate model of spirituality. When Constantine made Christianity legitimate and Christians were no longer martyred, convents began to be a choice for women to show their commitment to God. When the church allowed priests to marry, becoming a pastor's wife was an ideal sought after by many women. The missionary movement opened another door for women to show their love and zeal and so it became the preferred spiritual model.

It appears that culture has always shaped the church, although the truth of the New Testament has motivated some individuals to shape society. In light of the fact that various influences have changed the epitome of spirituality from physical martyr, to spiritual martyr and celibacy, to family life, the questions that emerge for women are: "What is the preferred model of spirituality today? What is the biblical basis for choosing a specific model of ministry? To what degree is a woman's choice of ministry influenced by the culture in which she lives and how much is it a sense of individual calling?"

This raises some other questions: Are women called to fulfill the great commission? Are they called to, "Go...and make disciples...teaching them....baptizing them...?" Or are they told they must find a man who will go with them so that they can serve under his headship? Or are they told to go and do all these things but not in the organized church where patriarchal hierarchy reigns? Or are women sent to "Samaria" but not permitted to fulfill the great commission in "Jerusalem"?

How much are the answers to these questions determined by culture and how much by Scripture?

Discussion and Reflection Questions

1. Is ministry a sexual role or a spiritual role? Does the female body make you different spiritually?

2. In the "made in the image of God" passages, is the focus on sexuality or humanity?

3. If Adam's sin of disobedience is fully redeemable by the blood of Christ, is not Eve's sin of being deceived also? If not, then women are mired forever in the fall, unable to move out into spiritual freedom and participate fully in both the blessings and the responsibilities of being "sons of God." What do you do with this inconsistency?

4. Does a wife sin if she does not submit to her husband but a husband not sin if he does not submit to his wife?

5. Why is it that women can so often do anything on the mission field: establish churches, lead and teach anyone but can only teach women and children in their home church?

6. Some passages are taken as imperatives for today and some are seen as culturally conditioned. Even some individual passages are inconsistently applied. How would you respond to the following:

    i. some who say that 1 Timothy 3 forbids women to be deacons will allow single men and married men without children to be deacons even though the same hermeneutic which excludes women ought to exclude these men.

    ii. some who say 1 Corinthians 14 forbids women to speak in church will say that 1 Corinthians 11 allows them to prophesy provided their heads are covered. How can they not speak and still prophesy?

    iii. some who say women cannot have authority would agree that women obviously have been given the gift of prophecy. Since prophecy is the most sought after, authoritative gift, how can women not have the power to use it authoritatively?

   iv. some who say 1 Timothy 2:12 means exactly what it says, then say, "It can't mean exactly what it says!" when they get to verse 15.

7. How does authority fit into the biblical idea of ministry?

8. On what basis did the early church give responsibility?

9. What did Jesus have to say about power? about service within the body? about hierarchy?

10. Does God call women as well as men to specific ministries?

11. Opportunities for women often include Christian education, assistant pastorships, parachurch leadership, evangelizing, teaching and writing, but usually exclude being senior pastor, preaching, distributing communion, and often ushering? On what basis is a distinction made between various forms of ministry?

12. Paul was concerned that the dress and manner of women not give offense. What offense are we giving to the world when we do NOT permit women the full use of their training and giftedness of leadership in the church?

13. How is the credibility of the church affected by the way it views women?

Chapter 5
IMPLEMENTING A RESPONSE

The challenge here is to respond with Biblical integrity

Christian women are experiencing a strange mixture of excitement, challenge and frustration as they seek to make sense out of the fact that they are experiencing a very clear sense of call while their giftedness and education as well as their leadership skills exercised in the workplace are not given credibility or affirmation within the Christian Church. This has a profound effect not only on the women themselves, but also on the church's testimony to the world. The church is seen as being restrictive rather than freeing - a perception that is diametrically opposed to the Good News we profess to proclaim.

But quite apart from how the church is perceived by the world, we must address the question of how God perceives the church. How well are we modeling the caring, nurturing community of redeemed men and women that Christ came to establish? The Christian community ought to be setting an example of the "kingdom" reality - the eschatological community that we will all experience someday, rather than model the kind of community that perpetuates sinful structures.

The challenge of being a Christian is to reveal Christ to the world. That means *His* values, *His* attitudes, *His* truth.

A study of history reveals how often we have headed off on a tangent of our own creation. We need to be honest about what Scripture reveals about the role of men and women in relationship with each other and with God. It's exciting to see men and women who are serious about the challenge of being a Christian in today's world, choose to set aside preconceived interpretations and grapple with the word of God in order to hear afresh God's voice of truth. Some will have their beliefs strengthened, others will be challenged to think differently. Our final goal is to discover how, with our differing interpretations, we can live out the ultimate mandate of unity within our churches.

How do we set both men and women free from stereotypes to live in response to God?

How do we change attitudes, laws and practices? The steps for being a change agent are as follows:[1]

    A. Develop a vision.

    B. Define beliefs that relate to that vision.

    C. Discern the present reality.

    D. Design goals to move from reality to vision.

    E. Determine available resources.

    F. Decide on the action.

    G. Do it and evaluate.

A. Develop a Vision

Visionaries, often called "paradigm pioneers" are those who see things differently.

A willingness to even look at a new paradigm is usually the result of some uneasiness, some disequilibrium, some sort of dissatisfaction with the way things are at present. The status quo - for some reason - becomes uncomfortable. Women are at that point now.

The process between that first step and making a paradigm shift may be a long slow one, or it may come in a sudden flash, but in order to actually shift paradigms, we must believe that a new vision will be better than what exists.

A place to begin creating a vision for how women are to function in the church is by asking, "What would the church look like if it built ministry around gifts?" What structures best suit the message that the Holy Spirit has called men and women to live in a community of believers and has gifted those men and women to build up one another into Christ as the head?

If the church were built around gifts, it would be:

- **a community** in which men and women carry out the tasks of the church life and participate equally in the decision making process.

- **a community** in which both men and women use their talents as delegates to the assemblies of church government.

- **a community** in which both men and women seek the wisdom of the Holy Spirit, which brings unity, rather than depending on the wisdom of human leaders which often brings division.

- **a community** in which the function, position and service of men and women is not based on their gender but upon their gifting and their Christian character so that they are all built up through teaching, preaching, tongues, prophetic word, administration, acts of service, shepherding, etc.

- **a community** in which both men and women understand that Christ is the head of the church, His body.
- **a community** in which mutual submission is practiced.

B. Define Beliefs Related to that Vision

There is a tension created in all of us whenever we are in a paradigm shift. The uneasiness that makes us consider a new paradigm in the first place is intensified by the fear of moving in the wrong direction. The very fact that a view is new, doesn't automatically make it right, but the fact that it challenges our present view doesn't make it wrong, either. And so there can be a struggle. We see problems with maintaining the status quo and yet we also see what happens when people move in a wrong direction simply because of blind trust in the leader. Many people follow a visionary into incredible error.

It is not enough, therefore, to simply trust someone else's vision but it is crucial to determine what criteria we use to allow the past to be pushed out of the way and discern the underlying assumptions upon which the new paradigm is based. Are they in fact true?

Only when beliefs are defined can you critique another's position. Only when beliefs are defined can you know whether the vision you have is Biblical. (See Appendix B for a summary of two contrasting belief systems.)

Don Posterski of World Vision International, says:[2]

- We all have a right and also a responsibility to define our beliefs and to stand by those beliefs.
- We need to confess that all our structures are subjective.
- We need to confess that some structures are more biblical than others.

Some restrictive structures are needed for immaturity and brokenness. But if they become institutionalized, like legalism, they remain immature, become infantile and keep people shackled.[3] Dominance models, power positions, self aggrandizement, lording it over one another - none of these is consistent with the One who laid down his life for His sheep.

The process of moving to a more biblical vision, regardless of what the vision relates to, is to list beliefs that relate to the vision and then determine if those beliefs are consistent and compatible with Scripture. In order to determine if the vision presented in this study regarding the basis for service and leadership within the church, is, in fact, more Biblical than the reality we live with, it is necessary to identify the beliefs that relate to this specific vision.

1. Beliefs Related to Controversial Definitions

While hermeneutics is definitely an issue, underlying those principles of interpretation is the issue of definitions. The concepts described by such words as ministry, leadership, headship, authority and submission all need clarification.

The controversial definitions are all resolved by the use of the paradigm of redemption to view Scripture and the model of community Jesus taught as the context in which the redeemed life is to be lived out.

If a theology of leadership is developed based on the model of the servant leadership of Christ, rather than on hierarchy and authority, there will be no theological problem with women responding to the call of God upon their lives and participating in any kind of ministry. When ministry is understood as service instead of power, and authority is recognized as being in the Word rather than in the person, there will be no problem with the hermeneutical issues, for the inconsistencies are all explainable within the broader context.

The issue of *headship* is settled by looking at the context of the passage rather than superimposing a standard meaning of "head" on all passages. The issue of *authority* is settled by the understanding of "authentein" as something quite other than "exousia." The issue of *submission* is settled by an understanding of mutual submission that is taught both in Scripture and in the model of community in which gifts were exercised by all.

2. Beliefs Related to Biblical Authority

According to Martin, authority has been interpreted as the right to command obedience, and in the Christian culture of the past twenty centuries, women promised to obey their husbands and the secular law permitted the husband to use physical force to carry out his authority.[4]

Martin says:

> lurking somewhere in the theology of women's submission is the idea that males and God have a special relationship. It does not lessen the pain that theologians confine the relationship to authority. Indeed this confines it to the worst possible place. For it is with their "authority" that men have ruled that women may not serve God in any way but that which fits their notion of what constitutes feminine behaviour.[5]

Today the strength of that position is weakening and Christians "soften the impact of authority...by giving the male ultimate responsibility....By this interpretation male authority becomes not a right but a service."[6] The use of the word "headship" is the term then used by the church to make male authority palatable to the modern Christian woman.[7] C. S. Lewis verbalizes this attitude when he says:

> It is painful, being a man, to have to assert the privilege, or the burden, which Christianity lays upon my own sex....It is an old saying that you salute the uniform not the wearer. Only one wearing the masculine uniform...can represent the Lord to the church. We men often make very bad priests. That is because we are insufficiently masculine.[8]

Martin has strong words to say about the principle of male authority: "It is a false teaching inserted into Christian theology by a male-dominated culture in love with authority"[9]

What, then, is the legitimate use of authority - biblically? And when does authority get abused?

Abuse of authority is inherent in any system which places one group of people in authority simply because they belong to that group. The solution is the biblical teaching of mutual submission and the use of gifts to determine function within the community.

Neither male nor female should have ultimate authority in a truly Christian community, for the role of the community is to discern God's will and God is the ultimate authority.[10]

3. Beliefs Related to Community

There are two levels of belief connected with community. First, it is important to acknowledge that God intended for us to live in community. Then it is important to discover what that community should look like.

God Intended Community

Grenz and Kjesbo would agree with Gilbert Bilezikian (see Chapter 1 pp.8-10) that God intends His people to live in, develop, and model community. They express it this way:

> God's goal of establishing community sets the context for a biblical understanding of the church....Our full participation in God's new community awaits the eschatalogical transformation of human life in the Kingdom of God. Nevertheless...we can partake of that eschatalogical fellowship now....In the midst of a broken world, our Lord calls us to mirror as much as possible that ideal community of love which reflects his own character....The church is to be the community in which [human] differences do not constitute the foundation of identity and activity....In the old order, people readily discriminated on the basis of sex. Christ's redemptive work however, frees us from the role of hierarchy as the fundamental

principle for male-female relationships....The New Testament commands us to live according to the vision of the new creation. This vision looks forward to a day of complete reconciliation among people of all races, every social standing and both genders. The task of the church is to allow this vision to transform the present reality....to point toward the perfect fellowship of God with humankind that will characterize God's eschatalogical reign....We must strive to reflect this vision in our present corporate life through structures that promote community and mutuality....Our appeal to the eschatalogical vision does not mean that we set the new creation over against the old. On the contrary, what God inaugurated in Christ's coming and will bring to consummation at our Lord's return is of one piece with what he began at creation. The call for full participation of men and women in the church is the fulfillment of God's egalitarian intention from the beginning, as indicated in the Genesis creation narratives.[11]

Characteristics of this Community

In order for a community to be healthy, it must have both unity and ministry. Often a group of Christians becomes so focused on building unity that they forget the purpose for which they are to maintain unity. On the other hand, some become so focused on the ministry that they neglect the need to build unity. Both are needed. And one necessary factor in facilitating both unity and ministry is accountability.

    a.   Unity means oneness - a total acceptance of each other. There can be no second class citizens. The structures of society around us have no relevance inside the church. The call is to overcome the worldly way of looking at gender, race and class.

    b.   Ministry means striving side by side for the gospel. We have become a Kingdom of Priests. There is a direct connection between oneness and the obligation to minister and there can be no authentic community without full participation of all members within the life and ministry of that community.

There is a tension that will probably always exist between God's call and the church's affirmation of the call, but some of that tension would be eased if we remembered that position simply permits and validates ministry. God calls us first and foremost to Himself and out of that relationship flows a call to ministry. The church then affirms the character and gift qualifications for that ministry by conferring title or position. Often, more importance is placed on the position a person is given than on the ministry to which they are called, the person's giftedness or their relationship with Christ which is primary.

c. Accountability means accepting responsibility and mutual submission within the community. Anyone who demands the freedom to exercise his or her gifts without being accountable to the community is not behaving as a Christian; therefore, women need to be sensitive, as do men, to the culture in which they serve. A woman is free to respond to God's call to ministry, but that call needs to be subject to the affirmation of the community - not because she is a woman but because she is, as are men, responsible and accountable to the Christian community to which she belongs.

4. Beliefs Related to Feminism

Feminism is raising questions about patriarchy, women's role in the church, the nature of God and the nature of the church - all of which need careful responses. Pat answers are not good enough. Some women are simply anti-church but others are genuinely seeking truth. It is important to not group all those who call themselves feminists into one category, and assume they all believe the same thing. There are various approaches to Scripture taken by those who call themselves feminists and in order for thoughtful dialogue to take place, we need to understand the differences.

Feminism: The movement toward equal rights, equal status, and equal opportunity for men and women in a male dominated culture.

Feminist: A person, male or female, who favours the abolishment of gender-based roles in society, the home and church. Within the category called feminist, there are many different spiritual beliefs represented.

Some are pagans involved in the worship of a female deity or goddess. Some are humanists who disallow God, revelation and religion in the discussion of feminism. Others operate within a Christian framework and believe that the writers of the Bible were simply men of their times who were limited in their perspectives. They may use a hermeneutic that sifts out anything that is offensive to women. Still others believe that the Bible is authoritative and must be understood in that light but also embrace the feminist ideal of abolishing gender-based roles in society, church and the home. In general, all feminists who seek to understand the role of women from a biblical perspective will argue that:

- The equality of women is affirmed by Scripture.
- Female subordination was a result of sin.
- Galatians 3:28 is not limited to their spiritual standing before God but refers to the practical working out of that standing in society.
- Mutual submission is taught by Ephesians 5:21-24
- Head does not mean "authority over" but "source of."
- Paul does not <u>teach</u> one thing and <u>practise</u> another.
- Scripture teaches that role is based on gifts rather than gender.

5. Beliefs Related to Giftedness

The Great Commission was given to the church as a whole which includes women as well as men. The Holy Spirit equips women as well as men with whatever gifts are needed to "make disciples, teach and baptize." That equipping, whether it be in the area of leadership, teaching, or ministry will include authority but it will not be authority "over" another but the authority "of" the Word and Spirit of God. Consequently:

- Gifts are not gender related.
- Specific calling is not determined by gender.

- Biology is not destiny: spiritual commitment is. True blessedness is open to single women and childless women as well as married women and men.
- God intended a unity when he created male and female.
- True unity negates hierarchy.
- Love, not legality, is the measure of God's followers.

6. Beliefs Related to Leadership

Collaborative leadership is the Biblical model: a leadership that is enabling, uplifting and empowering, not a leadership that is domineering.

The role of leadership is that of:

- creating a shared vision
- engaging others to fulfill that vision
- developing leaders
- multiplying leaders
- enabling others to effectively function in their area of giftedness
- encouraging others to find their unique ministry

Spiritual leadership requires those who:

> embody the character of Christ,
> embrace the vision of Christ and
> empower the people of Christ.[12]

Women can do these things. Woman, because she is made in the image of God, can reflect His love as fully as man and that is the essence of Spiritual leadership - not power and authority. The New Testament pattern seems to have been that of shared leadership, a responsibility held by a number of elders.

Women need to be on a leadership team because they can and do bring different perspectives to any situation. Women may not bring a unique perspective because they are women sexually, but because, as women, they have a different life experience. "If we do find ourselves with more shared leadership we will surely want to say...that whether a woman should run the team or not, if it has no women on it at all it is most certainly inadequate."[13]

The Church needs the unique qualities women bring to leadership and in order to incorporate those unique qualities, the style of Church leadership may need to change. Also, to exclude women simply because they are women is to impoverish our church. They have at least half of the giftedness God intended the church to have.

Leadership is not about authority and power - it is about being a follower of Christ and attracting others to follow him, too. It is about responsibility. It is about Jesus' command to feed his sheep.

7. Beliefs Related to Interpretive Principles

It is clear that there are many cultural beliefs and historical practices that affect the way we read Scripture: i.e.. John's account of foot washing (John 13:5-17) is usually interpreted as a cultural practice relating to the fact that people wore sandals. How many today follow the clear command of Jesus to wash one another's feet? Why not, when Jesus himself said that they ought to do it? Was the command only for the disciples? Only for that day? How do we know? On what basis do we make our decision? We need to be conscious of the paradigms and the principles we use to interpret Scripture.

It is not acceptable to reject portions of Scripture, although some portions are situation specific.

It is possible that we have been misreading Scripture.

It is necessary to revisit passages in light of cultural challenges; i.e. slavery, environmental issues.

8. Beliefs Related to Cultural Restrictions

Man and woman were both created to be relational, they were both to have dominion, they were both given the mandate to work and to procreate. Mary Stewart Van Leeuwen describes how the relationship is worked out: they were created to complement each other and were given freedom to structure that complementarity. How we structure it becomes our culture.[14]

We tend to make the mistake of accepting culture as God's mandate rather than man's creative way of living out the mandate of God. We replace God's creation order with human creation. Obviously sin enters into the structuring of our culture just as it enters into every area of life. Abuses abound, but those abuses are not ordered of God; they are rather humanity's distortion of the freedom given. Men and women abuse the cultural working out of complementarity by using gender roles as a means of power over each other, or making them legalistic and rigid, confining both men and women in predetermined functions.[15]

When Paul says, "in Christ there is neither male nor female," he is giving a principle that we are expected to live out - the principle that Christ came to do away with all the culturally developed distinctions, and the results of sin. This is the statement that takes us back to the creation order - a statement which does away with hierarchy rather than establishing it.

There is a difference, however, in refusing to allow culture to determine our theology and being sensitive to culture for the sake of the gospel.

The issue of how the freedom we have in Christ gets lived out in a specific culture is very important. And it is here that Paul's admonition is applicable: that while all things are permissible because of the freedom given to us in Christ, not all things are wise. So that while there is no theological reason why women should be excluded from any form of ministry: giving them the freedom or the right - they are also free to choose <u>not</u> to exercise that right so that others may not be offended. It is at this point that the culture in which each woman lives must be taken into consideration (which was the issue for the Corinthians). Culture includes the culture of denomination as well as race, gender, language and economic status.

This is where true humility and servanthood become evident. If women are truly seeking to serve their community of faith as well as the broader community, they need to maintain the delicate balance of personal freedom and submission to the community; of challenging tradition and honoring one another. They also need to be able to break new ground without running out of bounds, resist the status quo without being militantly aggressive. Women have the capacity to have this kind of sensitivity in the same way that men have - when they are aware that the expression of their ministry is channeled by God and not restricted by someone who wishes to have "authority" over them; that their ministry is restricted by their own choice rather than by exclusion on the basis of gender.

C. Discern the Present Reality

In order to bring about change, the obvious place to begin is where you are. People are only motivated to change by a discomfort of some sort - and when they see there is something in it for them.

What is the current situation? It is important to know the group that is being asked to change, to know their motivations and the source of their resistance, if any, and to discover their hidden agenda.

Where is the community in relation to the issue of the role of women? Are all members of the community starting from the same base? What limits will I need impose upon myself for the sake of the community? What changes in myself am I willing to make for the sake of the community? What are the cultural norms to which I must be sensitive?

D. Design Goals to Move from Reality to Vision

What do we want to accomplish? Different cultures will have different goals. Some will want to:

- change the church constitution to permit the ordination of qualified women.
- increase the number of women on Church committees in order to have their perspective included in all decision making.
- create a mentoring system which will encourage young women to grow and take responsibility.
- build community that is helpful and nurturing, not hurtful and diminishing.[16]

- discover if there is a female model of leadership.
- teach women to read and write.
- work toward eliminating economic slavery of women.
- advocate for land tenure for women.
- fight for inheritance rights, economic and legal rights for women.

Others will want to………???

E. Determine the Available Resources

These are the persons, things, events and activities that are available to draw on.

- what talents?
- what people in our community?
- what people outside our community?
- what materials - literature, tapes, videos, study materials?
- what occasions?
- what places?
- what funds?

How do we best use the strengths of women to change the situation for women? Women's strengths include:[17]

- vulnerability - leads to openness to growth and maturing
- connectedness - leads to ability to develop a strong network
- nurturing - leads to ability to nurture and empower others, which is the essence of leadership
- emotions - leads to being real
- cooperation - leads to finding strength and resources in community
- creativity - leads to finding solutions

F. Decide on the Action

1. Get ideas! Brainstorm, gather ideas from others, do research, consult strategy lists, consult experts. List anything that comes to mind.

2. Evaluate ideas.

    - Is this appropriate for us?
    - Is this appropriate for the specific situation?
    - Do we have the resources?
    - Do we have the time?
    - Are we willing to take the risk of doing it this way?

3. Choose the best ways - those ideas having the most "yeses"

4. Prioritize those ways according to determined criteria.

5. Plan implementation: ask what? why? when? who? where? how?

G. Do it...then evaluate and revise goals.

Discussion and Reflection Questions

1. Does gender determine ministry or does ministry flow out of call and giftedness? On what basis do you make this decision?

2. What inconsistencies in the teaching you have been given regarding women have you been able to identify through this study? Have they been resolved satisfactorily?

3. What vision have you developed for the way you live as the body of Christ?

4. What qualities and qualifications do you believe a leader must possess? Which of these, if any, are gender related?

5. Who do you need to cooperate with you in the designing of goals to move from your present reality to your vision?

6. What resources do you have available?

7. At the beginning of the study, you were asked to write down the issues you were bringing to this study so that you could return to them? What were those issues? What light has been shed on them for you? Which ones are still unresolved? Can you see what further steps you can take toward understanding and/or resolution?

8. What can you do personally to help make your community of faith more closely reflect the community that Stanley Grenz and Denise Muir Kjesbo describe (see page 103)?

EPILOGUE

We live in a community shattering world but the only hope for breaking down racial, class and gender barriers lies in community. If there is true community, there will be equality - for men and women of every race and class.

Who is going to model community? Will government, or the schools or business? No, only the church can, but the church needs to reclaim the Biblical model of community and begin to live it.

In this community, there is no room for anger at the past. We don't hear the angry voices of women in the New Testament wrangling with men over the years they were restricted. We don't hear the angry voices of men as they try to keep women "in their place." We don't hear angry voices at all. We just see men and women receiving the challenge of the gospel and moving out in the power of the Spirit to do whatever they were able to do in their culture in the name of Christ. By its very nature, community requires both mutual submission and mutual responsibility. We need, then, to work on this together so that both men and women are free to respond to God's call upon their lives. We need to work together to create a community that comes as close as we can make it to the community Christ taught about and sought to establish.

That is my vision - and as far as it relates to the role of men and women, I trust that this study has helped you shape your vision and provided you with some tools for moving your vision into reality.

The following analogy is one which can be used to illustrate in a graphic way the reality of how women are still bound by traditions and teachings that do not permit her the freedom to respond to the fullness of life that Jesus calls her to. Christ gives life. He is the life-giver. But He expects us all to participate in setting one another free to live that life fully.

This is not intended to be an exegesis of this passage of Scripture but simply to serve as a dramatic analogy.

John 11:1-44

Now a man named Lazarus was sick.....So the sisters sent word to Jesus...When he heard, Jesus said, "This sickness will not end in death".[and] He stayed where he was two more days....On his arrival, Jesus found that Lazarus had already been in the tomb for four days...."Take away the stone," he said.

"But, Lord," said Martha, the sister of the dead man, "by this time there is a bad odor, for he has been there four days."

Then Jesus said, "Did I not tell you that if you believed, you would see the glory of God?" So they took away the stone.

Jesus called in a loud voice, **"Lazarus, come out!"**

The dead man came out, his hands and feet wrapped with strips of linen, and a cloth around his face. Jesus said to them, **"Take off the grave clothes and let him go."**

Woman Be Free

The raising of Lazarus can serve as an appropriate analogy for us as women. We are hearing the voice - the loud voice of Jesus saying, "Woman, come out! Come out of the tomb - the place of death - the place that has imprisoned you - come out into life and freedom and the fullness of the abundant life to which I have called you. Woman, come out!"

And in obedience we <u>are</u> coming out - coming forth from the darkness of the tomb into the light of life - and yet we are finding our hands and feet and faces still bound by the grave clothes. We are unable to speak and to act because customs and attitudes of our society bind us into stereotypes - roles determined by others - not put there by God. And again we are hearing the voice - the loud voice of Jesus saying, "Take off the grave clothes and let her go!"

Only the voice of Jesus can call us forth from the tomb. He is the one who gives life. But he asks that we roll away the stone and unbind each other from the restrictive grave clothes that inhibit our freedom to live that new life. For that, we need each other. We need the community to be obedient so that, as individual women, we can follow the voice of our Master.

What is the Stone?

The stone is that which seals us into the tomb - the symbol of death, of non-existence. It is whatever says we are dead, interferes with our life, robs us of our identity.

We are commanded to roll away the stone - to give back to women the identity given to them by God.

It's easier to respond by saying, "There's a bad odor - she's been in the tomb too long!" Things have been this way for so long that it won't be pleasant to call her forth!!

Indeed, it won't be pleasant, or easy, because in order to give her back her identity - the identity ordained by God - we need to challenge the way societal values and historical practices have distorted the biblical teachings, relegating women to a secondary status and lowering her self-esteem. It won't be easy!

But Jesus speaks!

When Jesus calls, "COME FORTH!" who is this woman who emerges?

She, like the male, is made in the image of God. She, like the male, is redeemed by the blood of the Lamb, called into the royal priesthood, gifted by the Holy Spirit for the edifying of the body of Christ. She is one with man as the Bride of Christ - being purified and glorified - transformed into His likeness. She, like the man, is made in the image of God, to image Christ to a hurting world. Let us then obey the first command and roll away the stone that interferes with this God-given identity and allow her to "Come Forth."

The second command we may find even more difficult: to take off her grave clothes and let her go free - free to fulfill the destiny of her identity.

What are the Grave Clothes?

The grave clothes are those things which restrict her freedom, which bind her hands and feet and cover her face, preventing her from speaking and doing what she was called to say and do by her creator God.

They are those things imposed upon her by cultural practices which interfere in any way with the quality of life intended for her by a loving God.

They are those things which demean a woman's value - in her own eyes and in the eyes of others.

They are those attitudes, laws and practices which result in:

- exploitation
- violence
- sexual discrimination
- silence.

The woman created in the image of God, called forth by God and commissioned by God, needs to be set free to live with dignity and value.

If these are the grave clothes which we need to remove for women to be set free, how do we go about doing it?

CHANGE ATTITUDES

        CHANGE LAWS

                CHANGE PRACTICES

The Church Needs To Take Off The Grave Clothes!

First by seeing them

The church needs to acknowledge the reality of exploitation, injustice, violence and poverty within our own communities.

The church needs to acknowledge that violence is glorified in our society and acknowledge the extent to which it condones violence. Any system that requires submission of one group to another leads to the belief on the part of the group with "authority over" that whatever is required to ensure the submission of the other group is legitimate. It also allows for the group with "authority" to determine what submission looks like - to write the rules for the subordinate group and to determine the punishment for any lack of submission.

Sexism is the root cause of violence being directed toward women.

Then by taking action

The road to empowerment must be paved by those who have the power. Lazarus was brought to life by the voice of Jesus, but Jesus expected those standing by to become involved. They were the ones who had the power to set him free - to remove the restrictive grave clothes.

The goal of empowering WOMAN is to set her free to respond to the call of God upon her life. The goal of this study is to assist in taking off her grave clothes - those things which keep her bound and silent in a world that so desperately needs her voice, her gifts and her compassion.

Our goal is to break down barriers through encouragement, education and example.

Some of the barriers are theological beliefs which are being broken down by scholars who approach the Scripture with integrity, seeking to find what Scripture says rather than what they want it to say.

Some are attitudinal, borne out of the culture which makes women the subordinate class. These can only be broken down by those who have power being willing to give it up.

Christ is calling the church - both men and women - to be the church, His body. We cannot, DARE NOT, stand by and do nothing.

The church needs to begin to live as community. The personal lifestyle accepted by the church in many cultures is a privatized, individualized model which removes any accountability for what happens within the confines of one's own home - even if it involves emotional and physical abuse. The church needs to reject that model and begin to live the kind of community that Christ came to establish.

A Christian community operates on mutual submission, respect, building up of one another, challenging one another, caring for one another, sharing with one another. In a truly Christian community there will be no violence, no exploitation, no injustice, no exclusion based on gender, social status, or race.

We can learn to live with a theology of covenant and mutuality. We can change decision-making systems such as church committees and governments and function with men and women in leadership positions.

In a Christian community, men and women will work together to remove the obstacles in the way of women's full participation. Men and women can pool resources, be creative, learn from each other and support one another to restore the dignity of those on the margins of our society. If this is done, the church will distinguish itself as a compassionate and humane community which honours the name of Christ.

And in doing so, the church will address the reality of the fear that women live with - *FEAR IS THE BAD ODOR!* It is a woman's reality that many men do not understand. Fearful women are usually seen as neurotic, paranoid, somehow not quite in touch with reality. But unfortunately it IS their reality. Hopelessness is fear's companion, and anger is often the only tool women have with which to fight their fear and hopelessness. But when women attempt to use their anger, it is in turn used against them as justification for the violence they experience or for disregarding their concerns. Instead, we want to enlist the anger of men, too, against the injustices of society that allow one half of the human race to live as second class citizens while they have the power to call them into equality - call them into freedom - call them into the shared relationship for which they were created, to fulfill the destiny inherent in being made in the image of God.

God has given men and women together the power to change the world. Let's call one another to share that power and use our energy to work alongside one another.

Together, let's challenge the church to allow women to point out the injustices, and then listen - listen carefully - to their muffled cries and their screams of pain, even if they are couched in shouts of anger.

The church is called to be obedient to the voice of Jesus. We can be. We can hear the loud voice of Jesus. We can begin to remove the grave clothes and allow women to fulfill the destiny of their identity.

Let us together begin to make

"His Kingdom come —on EARTH as it is in Heaven."

ENDNOTES

Chapter 1 Introducing the Study

[1] Rebecca Merrill Groothuis, *Good News for Women*, (Grand Rapids: Baker Book House, 1997), p. 194

[2] W.Ward Gasque, "The Role of Women in the Church, in Society and in the Home," <u>Priscilla Papers</u>, Volume 2, Number 2 (Spring 1988), p.10

[3] This is not intended to be a comprehensive list of hermeneutical principles but only those applicable to this study. For a comprehensive treatment of the whole issue of interpretation, see *How to Read the Bible For All Its Worth* by Gordon D. Fee and Douglas Stuart, (Zondervan Publishing House: Grand Rapids, 1982)

Chapter 2 Investigating Paradigms

[1] Phyllis Trible, *God and the Rhetoric of Sexuality*, (Philadelphia: Fortress Press, 1978), p.98

[2] Gilbert Bilezikian, lecture, "Reclaiming Biblical Community," Wheaton Illinois: Christians for Biblical Equality Conference, July 1993

[3] Bilezikian, lecture, 1993

[4] Bilezikian, lecture, 1993

[5] Bilezikian, lecture, 1993

[6] Stanley Grenz and Denise Muir Kjesbo, *Women in the Church*, (InterVarsity Press: Downers Grove, 1995), p.211

[7] Faith Martin, *Call Me Blessed*, (Grand Rapids, Michigan: Eerdmans Publishing, 1998), p.73

Chapter 3a
Interpreting Scripture - Old Testament

[1] Mary Hayter, *The New Eve in Christ,* (Grand Rapids: Eerdmans Publishing House, 1987), p.102

[2] Trible, p.90

[3] Mary Hayter quotes J.I. Packer who makes this statement in, "I Believe in Women's Ministry," *Why Not?* edited by R.T. Beckwith (Abingdon Press, 1976), p.101

[4] Aida Besancon Spencer, *Beyond The Curse: Woman Called To Ministry*, (Nashville, Tennessee: Thomas Nelson, 1985), p.27

[5] Marion Taylor, lecture at Ontario Theological Seminary, 1992

[6] Spencer, p.29

[7] James Strong lists the following meanings for the Hebrew word *dabaq*: to impinge, i.e. cling or adhere; fig. to catch by pursuit: - abide fast, cleave, (fast together), follow close (hard after), be joined (together), keep (fast), overtake, pursue hard, stick, take. "A concise Dictionary of the Words in The Hebrew Bible," *The New Strong's Concordance* (Nashville: Thomas Nelson Publishers, 1984), p.29

[8] Mary J. Evans, *Woman in the Bible,* (Downers Grove: InterVarsity Press, 1983), p.19

[9] Taylor, lecture, 1992

[10] George Knight III, *The New Testament Teaching on the Role Relationship of Men and Women,* (Grand Rapids: Baker, 1977), p.32

[11] Knight, p.32

[12] Trible, p.128

[13] Gretchen Gaebelein Hull, "A New Testament Perspective on the Treatment of 'Everywoman'" *Priscilla Papers,* Volume 9, Number 2, (Spring 1995), p.9

[14] Hull, p.10

[15] Hull, p.11

[16] Spencer, p.42

[17] Martin, pp.99-100

[18] Martin, p.98

[19] Martin, p.99

[20] Grace May, "Who's Who? Biblical Models of Women in Leadership," *Priscilla Papers* Volume 7 Number 2, (Spring 1993), p.3

[21] John T. Willis, "Women in the Old Testament," *Essays on Women in Earliest Christianity*, edited by Carroll D. Osburn (Joplin Missouri: College Press, 1993), p.35

[22] Martin, p.94

[23] Martin, p.39

[24] Martin, p.39

Chapter 3b
Interpreting Scripture - New Testament

[1] Ben Witherington III, *Women and the Genesis of Christianity*, (Cambridge, Illinois: Cambridge University Press, 1990), p.9.

[2] Leonard Swidler, *Biblical Affirmations of Women*, (Philadelphia: The Westminster Press, 1979), p.154

[3] Swidler, p.154

[4] Swidler, p.156

[5] Swidler, p.156

[6] Swidler, pp.154-157

[7] Swidler, p.155

[8] Witherington, p.7

[9] Witherington, p.7

[10] Ruth Tucker and Walter Liefeld, *Daughters of the Church*, (Grand Rapids: Zondervan Publishing House, 1987), p. 29

[11] Lesley F. Massey, *Women and the New Testament*, (Jefferson, North Carolina: McFarland and Company, 1989), p.6

[12] Evans, p.53

[13] Gilbert Bilezikian, *Beyond Sex Roles*, (Grand Rapids: Baker Book House, 1985), p.102

[14] Grace May, "Who's Who: New Testament Female Ministry Role Models" *Priscilla Papers*, Volume 7 Number 3 (Summer 1993), p.5

[15] Swidler, p.145

[16] Spencer, p.57

[17] Spencer, p.60

[18] Spencer, p.61

[19] Bilezikian, p.85

[20] Evans, p.46

[21] Evans, p.52

[22] May, p.4

[23] May, p.5

[24] Grenz and Ksjebo, p.76

[25] Swidler, p.196

[26] Tucker, p.64

[27] Lawrence O. Richards, *Expository Dictionary of Bible Words*, (Grand Rapids: Zondervan, 1985), p. 505

[28] Bristow, p.xi

[29] Bristow, p.ix

[30] Bristow, p.x

[31] Tucker, p.66

[32] Roberta Hestenes made this statement in a question and answer session of the "New Patterns for Christian Women in Leadership" Conference, Toronto, 1989

[33] Tucker quotes F. F. Bruce, p.453

[34] Grenz and Kjesbo, p.177

[35] Hull, from video tape of lecture at Christians for Biblical Equality conference, 1993

[36] Gasque, p.9

[37] Martin, p.169

[38] Bilezikian as quoted by Katherine Haubert in *Women as Leaders*, (Monrovia, California: Marc Pub. 1993), footnote #71, p.87

[39] Haubert, p.41

[40] Haubert, p.41-42

[41] James Hurley, *Man and Woman in Biblical Perspective* (Grand Rapids: Zondervan, 1981), p.167

[42] Haubert quotes Gordon Fee, footnote #73, p. 87

[43] Hurley, p.173

[44] Martin, p.167

[45] Martin, p.167

[46] Anne Atkins, *Split Image*, (London: Hodder and Stoughton, 1987), p.110

[47] Atkins, p.109

[48] Grenz and Ksjebo, p.192

[49] Tucker, p.451

[50] Bristow, pp.62-63

[51] Haubert, p.62

[52] Bristow, p. 63

[53] Atkins, p.111

[54] Haubert, p.63

[55] Haubert, p.61

[56] Spencer, p.118

[57] Swidler, p.310

[58] Swidler, p.310

[59] Swidler, p.310

[60] Swidler, p.310

[61] Bilezikian, p.243

[62] Bilezikian, p.292

[63] Bilezikian, p.158

[64] Bilezikian, p.246

[65] Atkins, p.174

[66] Bilezikian, p.154

[67] Bilezikian, p.154

[68] Bilezikian, p.154

[69] Bristow, p.39

[70] Bristow, p.40

[71] Bristow, p.42

[72] Bristow, p.43

[73] Bristow, p.43

[74] Craig Keener, *Paul Women and Wives*, (Peabody Massachusetts: Hendrickson Publishers, 1992), p.135

[75] Atkins, p.123

[76] Bristow, p.71

[77] Bristow, pp.70-71

[78] Bristow, p.71

[79] Spencer, p.87

[80] Bristow, p.72

[81] Knight, p.18

[82] Knight, p.18

[83] Knight, p.19

[84] Bristow, p.74

[85] Catherine Kroeger made this statement on a video filmed at a conference of Christians for Biblical Equality, Wheaton, USA, 1993

[86] Bristow, p.75

[87] Bristow, p.75

[88] Bristow, pp.76-77

[89] Bristow, p.54

[90] Bristow, p.55

[91] Bristow, p.58

[92] Bilezikian, p.191

[93] Bilezikian, p.189

[94] Bilezikian, p.192

[95] Martin, p.50

Chapter 4 Identifying the Cultural Influences

[1] Swidler, pp.155-157

[2] Spencer, p.44

[3] Adriana Valerio, "Women in Church History," *Women: Invisible in Church and Theology*. Edited by Elisabeth Schussler Fiorenza and Mary Collins. (Edinburgh: T and T Clark Ltd., 1985), p.63

[4] Martin, p.19

[5] Martin, p.20

[6] Tucker, p.103

[7] Martin, p.20

[8] Martin, p.21

[9] Valerio, p.63

[10] Bristow, p.112

[11] Bristow, p.118-119

[12] Bristow, pp.112-113

[13] Martin, p.49

[14] Bristow, p.115

[15] Bristow, p.117

[16] Tucker, p.165

[17] Tucker, p.165

[18] Martin, pp.21-22

[19] Tucker, p.173

[20] Tucker, p.174

[21] Tucker and Liefeld, p.175

[22] Martin, p.81

[23] Martin, p.81

[24] Tucker and Liefeld, p.179

[25] Tucker and Liefeld, p.179

[26] Martin, p.25

[27] Tucker, p.252

[28] Martin, p.18

[29] Martin, p.27

[30] The material presented here is from a lecture entitled, "Subordination in the Godhead: A Re-Emerging Heresy," by Gilbert Bilezikian, Wheaton, USA: Christians for Biblical Equality Conference, 1993

[31] Martin, p.52

[32] W. Ward Gasque, "Biblical Manhood and Womanhood - Stressing the differences," *Priscilla Papers,* Volume 4, Number 1 (Winter, 1990), p. 9

[33] Gasque, p.9

Chapter 5 Implementing a Response

[1] In outlining this process, I am indebted to Joan D. Flikkema who wrote, "Strategies for Change: Being a Christian Change Agent," published in *Women, Authority and the Bible*, edited by Alvera Mickelsen, (Downers Grove, Illinois: InterVarsity Press, 1986), pp.256-274. Although I have adapted it for this study, the ideas and structure as well as the inspiration to become a change agent all come from this author. I have found the steps she presents to be extremely helpful in a variety of planning situations.

[2] Don Posterski, World Vision International, spoke at a Consultation on Women in Ministry sponsored by Evangelical Fellowship of Canada, Toronto, 1992

[3] Bilezikian, "Reclaiming Biblical Community," lecture, 1993

[4] Martin, p.54

[5] Martin, p.179

[6] Martin, p.54

[7] Martin, p.54

[8] Martin quotes C.S. Lewis, p.102

[9] Martin, p.55

[10] Atkins, p.137

[11] Grenz and Ksjebo, pp.175-179

[12] David McKenna, *Power to Follow, Grace to Lead*, (Dallas: Word, 1989), p.194

[13] Atkins, p.143

[14] Mary Stewart Van Leeuwen, lecture at CBE Conference, Wheaton, 1993

[15] Van Leeuwen, CBE Conference, 1993

[16] Miranda Lau, Chaplain Etobicoke General Hospital, used this phrase in a lecture in the Women in Ministry course at Ontario Theological Seminary, Toronto, 1989

[17] Jean Baker Miller, *Toward a New Psychology of Women*, (Boston: Beacon, 1986), Chapter 4, pp.29-48

BIBLIOGRAPHY

Adams, Q.M. *Neither Male Nor Female: A Study of the Scriptures.* Great Britain: Arthur H. Stockwell Ltd., 1973.

Alsdurf, James and Phyllis. *Battered into Submission.* Downers Grove, Illinois: InterVarsity Press, 1989.

Atkins, Anne. *Split Image.* London: Hodder and Stoughton, 1987.

Bilezikian, Gilbert. *Beyond Sex Roles.* Grand Rapids, Michigan: Baker Book House, 1985.

_____. Lecture: "Reclaiming Biblical Community," Christians for Biblical Equality Conference, Wheaton, Illinois: July, 1993.

_____. Lecture: "Subordination in the Godhead: A Re-Emerging Heresy," Christians for Biblical Equality Conference, Wheaton, Illinois: July, 1993.

Bristow, John Temple. *What Paul Really Said About Women.* San Francisco: Harper & Row, 1988.

Clouse, Bonnidell and Robert G. *Women In Ministry: Four Views.* Downers Grove, Illinois: InterVarsity Press, 1989.

Cunningham, Loren, David Joel Hamilton and Janice Rogers. *Why not Women?* Seattle, USA: YWAM Publishing, 2000.

Evans, Mary J. *Woman in the Bible.* Downers Grove, Illinois: InterVarsity Press, 1983.

Flikkema, Joan D. "Strategies for Change: Being a Christian Change Agent," *Women, Authority and the Bible,* Chapter 11, edited by Alvera Mickelsen. Downers Grove, Illinois: InterVarsity Press, 1986.

Fortune, Marie. *Is Nothing Sacred?* San Francisco: Harper and Row, 1989.

Gasque, W. Ward. "The Role of Women in the Church, in Society, and in the Home," *Priscilla Papers*, Volume 2, Number 2, (Spring, 1988), pp. 1-2, 8-10.

_____. "Biblical Manhood and Womanhood: Stressing the Differences," *Priscilla Papers*, Volume 4, Number 1, (Winter, 1990), page 9.

Grenz, Stanley. *Created for Community*. Wheaton, Illinois: Victor Books/Scripture Press Publications, 1996.

Grenz, Stanley & Denise Muir Kjesbo. *Women in the Church*. Downers Grove, Illinois: InterVarsity Press, 1995.

Gundry, Patricia. *Neither Slave Nor Free: Helping Women Answer the Call to Church Leadership*. San Francisco: Harper & Row Publishers, 1987.

Hassey, Janette. *No Time for Silence*. Grand Rapids: Academic Books, 1986.

Hayter, Mary. *The New Eve in Christ*. Grand Rapids, Michigan: Eerdmans Publishing Co., 1987.

Haubert, Katherine M. *Women as Leaders*. Monrovia, California: Marc, World Vision, 1993.

Hestenes, Roberta. "Women In Leadership: Finding Ways To Serve The Church," *Christianity Today*. October 3, 1986, pp. 5-10.

_____. Lecture, New Patterns for Christian Women in Leadership Conference, Toronto, Canada, 1989.

Hull, Gretchen Gaebelein. *Equal To Serve*. Old Tappan, New Jersey: Fleming H. Revell Co., 1987.

_____. "A New Testament Perspective on the Treatment of 'Everywoman'," *Priscilla Papers*, Volume 9, Number 2, (Spring, 1995).

_____. Video Lecture: "The Sin of Patriarchy," Christians for Biblical Equality Conference, Wheaton, Illinois: July, 1993.

Johnston, Robert K. "Biblical Authority and Interpretation: The Test Case of Women's Role in the Church and Home," *World Christian*, (Summer, 1990), pp. 32-35.

_____. "The Role of Women in the Church and Home: An Evangelical Testcase In Hermeneutics," *Scripture, Tradition and Interpretation*, edited by Ward Gasque. Grand Rapids, Michigan: Eerdman's Publishing Co., 1978, pp. 234-259.

Keener, Craig S. *Paul, Women and Wives*. Peabody, Massachusetts: Hendrickson Publishers, 1992.

Kroeger, Catherine Clark. Lecture, Christians for Biblical Equality Conference, Wheaton, Illinois: July, 1993.

Kroeger, Richard Clark and Catherine Clark Kroeger. *I Suffer Not a Woman*. Grand Rapids, Michigan: Baker Book House, 1992.

Liefeld, Walter L. "Women and the Nature of Ministry," *Journal of the Evangelical Theological Society*. (March, 1987), pp. 49-61.

Longenecker, Richard N. "Authority, Hierarchy & Leadership Patterns In The Bible," *Women, Authority & The Bible*, edited by Alvera Mickelsen. Downers Grove, Illinois: InterVarsity Press, 1986.

May, Grace. "Who's Who? Biblical Models of Women in Leadership," *Priscilla Papers*, Volume 7, Number 2, (Spring, 1993), pp. 1-5.

_____. "Who's Who: New Testament Female Ministry Role Models," *Priscilla Papers*, Volume 7 Number 3 (Summer, 1993), pp. 4-8.

Martin, Faith. *Call Me Blessed: The Emerging Christian Woman*. Grand Rapids, Michigan: Eerdmans Publishing Co., 1988.

Massey, Lesly F. *Women and the New Testament: An Analysis of Scripture in Light of the New Testament Era Culture*. Jefferson, North Carolina: McFarland and Company, 1989.

McKenna, David L. *Power to Follow, Grace to Lead*. Dallas, Texas: Word, 1989.

Mickelsen, Berkeley and Alvera. "Does Male Dominance Tarnish Our Translations?" *Christianity Today*, (October 5, 1979), pp. 23-29.

_____. "How Do We Interpret The Bible?" *World Christian*, (Summer 1990), pp. 28-31.

Miller, Jean Baker. *Toward a New Psychology of Women*. Boston: Beacon Press, 1976.

Osburn, Carroll D., editor. *Essays on Women in Earliest Christianity*. Joplin, Missouri: College Press, 1993.

Richards, Lawrence O. *Expository Dictionary of Bible Words*. Grand Rapids, Michigan: Zondervan Publishing House, 1985.

Schmidt, Alvin John. *Veiled And Silenced: How Culture Shapes Sexist Theology*. Macon, Georgia: Mercer University Press, 1989.

Spencer, Aida Besancon. *Beyond The Curse: Woman Called To Ministry*. Nashville, Tennessee: Thomas Nelson, 1985.

Stackhouse Jr., John. "Women in Public Ministry in the 20th-Century Canadian Evangelicalism: Five Models," *Studies in Religion*, Vol. 17, No 4, (Fall, 1988), pp. 471-485.

Storkey, Elaine. *What's Right With Feminism*. Grand Rapids, Michigan: Eerdmans Publishing Co., 1986.

Swartley, Willard M. *Slavery, Sabbath, War & Women: Case Issues in Biblical Interpretation*. Waterloo, Ontario: Herald Press, 1983.

Swidler, Leonard. *Biblical Affirmations of Woman*. Philadelphia: The Westminster Press, 1979.

Taylor, Marion. Lecture, "Women in the Old Testament," Women in Ministry Course, Toronto: Ontario Theological Seminary, 1992.

Trible, Phyllis. *God and the Rhetoric of Sexuality*. Philadelphia, USA: Fortress Press, 1978.

Tucker, Ruth A. and Walter Liefeld. *Daughters of the Church*. Grand Rapids, Michigan: Zondervan Publishing House, 1987.

Tucker, Ruth A. *Women in the Maze*. Downers Grove, Illinois: InterVarsity Press, 1992.

Valerio, Adriana. "Women in Church History," *Women: Invisible in Church and Theology*, edited by Elisabeth Schussler Fiorenza and Mary Collins. Edinburgh: T. and T. Clark Ltd., 1985.

Van Leeuwen, Mary Stewart. *Gender and Grace*. Downers Grove, Illinois: InterVarsity, 1990.

_____. Lecture, "Principalities, Powers and Gender Relations," Wheaton, Illinois: Christians for Biblical Equality Conference, July, 1993.

Willis, John T. "Women in the Old Testament" *Essays on Women in Earliest Christianity*, edited by Carroll D. Osburn. Joplin, Missouri: College Press, 1993, Chapter 2.

Witherington III, Ben. *Women and the Genesis of Christianity*. Cambridge, Illinois: Cambridge University Press, 1990.

Hierarchical Position

Hurley, James B. *Man and Woman in Biblical Perspective*. Leicester, England: InterVarsity Press, 1981.

Piper, John and Wayne Grudem. *Recovering Biblical Manhood and Womanhood*. Wheaton, Illinois: Crossway Books, 1991.

Knight, George W. III. *The New Testament Teaching on the Role Relationship of Men and Women*. Grand Rapids, Michigan: Baker Book House, 1977.

APPENDIX A

Glossary of Definitions

authentein - a word used only once in Scripture. Its extra-biblical usage varies but may have sexual connotations and suggests domineering and murder, or possibly source, as in "author."

authority - the power to determine, adjudicate or settle issues or disputes; jurisdiction, right to control, command or determine; power or right to direct the actions of others, to command and to punish for violations.

chain of command - a philosophical concept taken from the Ancient Greek worldview in which all forms of life were ranked in relation to each other according to their value. A hierarchy with the highest worth at the top and lowest at the bottom resulted. Beginning with animals and moving up we have women and slaves, then men, then gods.

chauvinist - a person who in a prejudiced way believes in the superiority of his or her own group. A "male chauvinist" assumes an innate male superiority in most areas of life.

complementarity* - the state or quality of being that serves to fill out or complete; mutually supplying each other's lack. It does not suggest sameness.

culture* - the customary beliefs, social forms, and material traits of a racial, religious or social group.

deacon - from the Greek word *diakonos* which is variously translated minister, servant or deacon. The focus is clearly that of a loving service.

egalitarianism* - from French *egal* meaning equal. A belief in human equality especially with respect to social, political and economic rights and privileges.

elders - from the Greek word *presbyteros*. They were the ones in the early church who directed the affairs of the church. Some preached and taught, but they were all chosen carefully according to specific moral and personal criteria.

equality - a moral concept, the value and measure of rightness that justice respects; a theist presupposes that all [person] are equal in terms and rights connected with their God-given common nature and dignity as persons.

'ezer - this is the Hebrew word which is translated "helper" and is used by hierarchalists to infer a position of subordination for Eve (the helper) and thus for all women and consequently a position of authority for Adam (the one being helped) and thus for all men. The frequent use, however, in the OT to refer to God negates any meaning of subordination and the fact that *'ezer* is modified by *knegdo* meaning "face to face" or "equivalent to" rules out any idea of superiority on the part of this human helper.

feminine/masculine - those qualities and characteristics of behaviour that are assigned by a specific culture to be appropriate for women/men.

giftedness - the basis upon which an individual's function within the community of the early church was determined. The purpose was the building up of the body as all the ligaments and joints worked together with Christ, the source and giver of the life of the body (Christ, the head).

gender - a classification of language that designates the sex of the person to which it refers: i.e. humanity, people, parent, child, they, persons and individual are clearly not gender-specific words; whereas male, female, brothers, sisters, her, she, mother, father, son and daughter are clearly gender specific. The confusion comes with such words as "man" and "he" which once were inclusive of both sexes but now are seen by many as gender specific and thus include only those of the male sex when used.

headship - the word "headship" does not appear in Scripture but is a term used by many to refer to the authority of the male over the female (or perhaps only the husband over the wife). It comes from Paul's figurative use of the word *kephale* meaning "head." Scholars disagree but it is generally accepted that it can have a variety of meanings including leader, first, origin, etc. and therefore it can only be the context which clarifies its meaning.

helper - see *'ezer* above.

hermeneutics - the branch of theology that prescribes rules and guidelines by which the Bible should be interpreted.

hierarchy* - a ranking which places each person or thing subordinate to the one above it.

inclusive language - the use of words which are not gender specific when the intention is to include both men and women.

leadership - making a difference in the world through and with other people - takes many forms and is not tied to status or title. Often the designated leader is not a leader at all.

ministry - any act of service for the benefit, exaltation or edification of others, either Christians or non-Christians, motivated by Christ's love. It is the calling of all the people of God.

ministries - specific tasks taken up to serve the church. Pastoring is one of the ministries of the church, not THE ministry.

mutuality - a state in which feelings, position or assets are shared equally. It connotes a partnership with equality.

naming - providing a word or phrase which designates a specific identity for a person or thing.

order of creation - the timing of the events of creation in terms of first to last.

ordination - to officially set aside a person for specific service.

partnership - the state or condition of sharing a joint venture, including risks and profits.

paradigm - a term used to identify the model, pattern or the framework through which we view and therefore interpret something.

patriarchy* - a social organization marked by the supremacy of the father in the clan or family, the legal dependence of the wife and children, and the reckoning of descent and inheritance in the male line.

power over - the possession of authority, influence or control over another.

preferred spiritual model# - the ideal way in which women could live out their spirituality. This has changed through the years. For early Christians, martyrdom was elevated. Then came celibacy. Priesthood was not available for women, but the convent provided an alternative and also the opportunity for an education. When clergy were allowed to marry, the role of a minister's wife became the ideal. More recently the missionary movement provided the model for real dedication for women.

priesthood - an order established in the OT which consisted of only males of the tribe of Levi. They demonstrated the need for a mediator -- a role fulfilled by Jesus (Heb.7). In the NT, Christians are called "a royal priesthood" (1 Peter 2:9), and a "kingdom of priests" (Rev. 1:5; 5:10). There is no indication that this refers only to men, but includes all believers.

prophesy - to prophesy is to speak for another. A prophet is a person authorized to speak for another as Moses and other OT prophets were authorized to speak for God. Women as well as men might serve as God's spokespersons. But this role, unlike kingship and priesthood was not hereditary. God calls whom he desires.

secular feminist - a person who believes in feminism but who has no Christian or scriptural basis for the belief.

sexism* - prejudice or discrimination based on sex; attitude or behaviour based on traditional stereotypes of sexual roles; discrimination or a devaluation based on a person's gender.

sex* - the division and distinguishing of organisms into male and female categories. The total of the structural, functional, and behavioral characteristics of living beings that distinguishes them as male or female

silence* - the absence of speech, noise or sound.

subordination* - placed in or occupying a lower class or rank; differs from submission in that anyone may choose to be in submission to another, but a subordinate person is by definition always under the authority of someone else.

submission+ - to attach to or identify with another; the accommodation of disparate wills.

veiled - isolation of women from the observation by, or interaction with, any male other than her husband.

* Webster's New Collegiate Dictionary, (Springfield Mass: G. & C. Merriam Company, 1980)

+ Kevin Quast, New Testament Professor, Ontario Theological Seminary, lecture, 1992

Ann Jervis, Professor, Wycliffe College, Toronto, lecture 1992

APPENDIX B

Two Different Paradigms

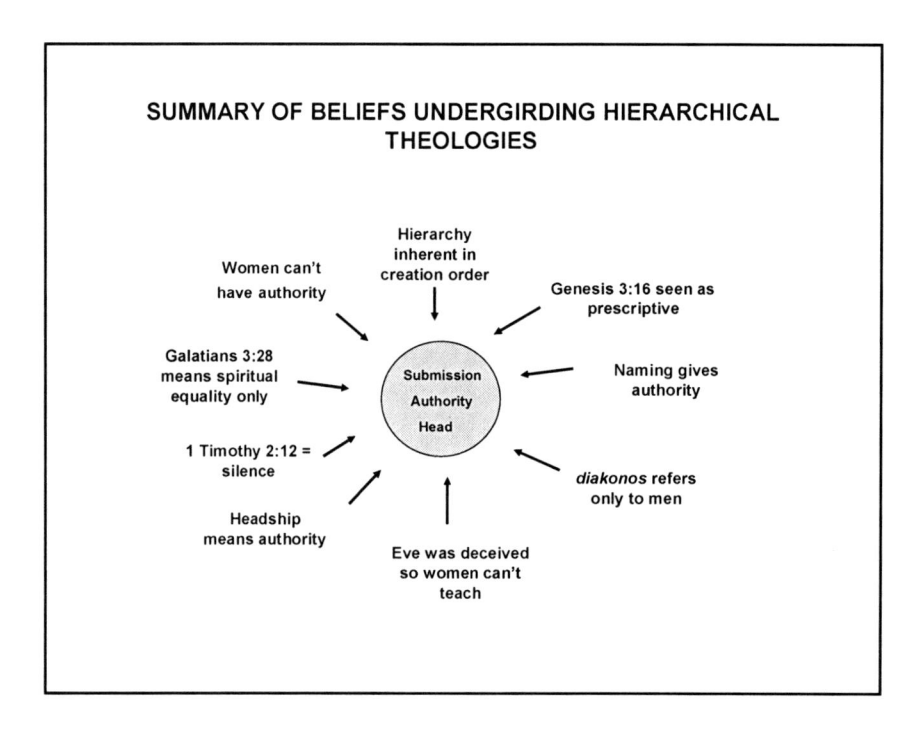

SUMMARY OF BELIEFS UNDERGIRDING HIERARCHICAL THEOLOGIES

- Hierarchy inherent in creation order
- Women can't have authority
- Genesis 3:16 seen as prescriptive
- Galatians 3:28 means spiritual equality only
- Naming gives authority
- 1 Timothy 2:12 = silence
- *diakonos* refers only to men
- Headship means authority
- Eve was deceived so women can't teach

Center: Submission / Authority / Head

Figure 5

In this paradigm, the following meanings prevail:

'ezer knegdo	"helper equal to" means subordinate
kephale	head means authority
authentein	translated authority
sigao	means cannot speak
hupotasso	means submission of the wife to the husband and then is carried over into the church to mean submission of the women to the men

There are 3 core texts:

>Ephesians 5:22 – submission
>1 Timothy 2:15 - I do not permit
>Ephesians 5:23 and 1 Corinthians 11:3 - head

Galatians 3:28 is understood to have spiritual meaning, but not to have any impact on the current behaviour.

The application is that woman is subject to the man as Christ is subject to the Father. Generally, traditionalists will say that women are not inferior to men, but that while they are equal spiritually, they do not have equal spiritual authority. That is to say, their function within the body of Christ is based on their gender. The Biblical basis for that is the belief that head means authority and since Christ is the head (authority) of the church and man is the head (authority) of the woman, she is to be submissive and cannot have authority over the man. Therefore, she cannot teach men or preach the word.

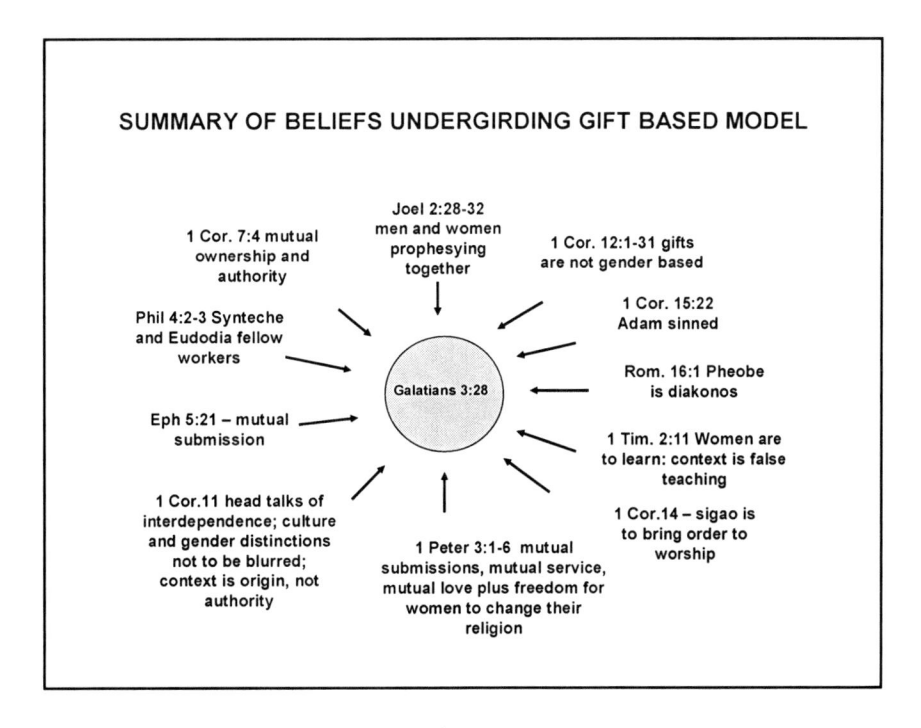

SUMMARY OF BELIEFS UNDERGIRDING GIFT BASED MODEL

Surrounding Galatians 3:28:

- 1 Cor. 7:4 mutual ownership and authority
- Joel 2:28-32 men and women prophesying together
- 1 Cor. 12:1-31 gifts are not gender based
- Phil 4:2-3 Synteche and Eudodia fellow workers
- 1 Cor. 15:22 Adam sinned
- Rom. 16:1 Pheobe is diakonos
- Eph 5:21 – mutual submission
- 1 Tim. 2:11 Women are to learn: context is false teaching
- 1 Cor.11 head talks of interdependence; culture and gender distinctions not to be blurred; context is origin, not authority
- 1 Peter 3:1-6 mutual submissions, mutual service, mutual love plus freedom for women to change their religion
- 1 Cor.14 – sigao is to bring order to worship

Figure 6

In this second paradigm, the following meanings prevail:

'ezer knegdo	helper "equal to" means face to face, suitable to
kephale	head means source
authentein	is recognized as an unusual word which suggests dominance
sigao	means voluntary silence in order to pay attention
hupotasso	is a voluntary submission and is used in the context of mutual submission

There is one core text: Galatians 3:28, which summarizes the equality of all people in Christ and has both spiritual and practical implications because the daily living out of our identity in Christ can never be separated from the eternal reality of our life in Him.

Men and women are equally created in the image of God, to live together in community and serve within that community on the basis of their giftedness by the Holy Spirit. Service within the community is not determined by gender. The essence of community is mutual submission and mutual responsibility: each one is to be a servant, contributing to the building up of each other according to their gifts.

ABOUT THE AUTHOR

Lynn Smith

A school teacher by profession, Lynn served Tyndale University College and Seminary in Toronto, Canada, as Dean of Students and Vice President of Student Development where leadership development became the focus of her involvement with students. It was during this time that she first began to be aware of the significance of the Church's teaching regarding the role of women. As students shared their struggles around this issue, she realized the necessity for her own personal study in order to sort out what was "Scriptural" and what was "Tradition."

Her study resulted in the writing of *Gender or Giftedness* which has now been translated into German, French, Arabic, and Croatian and has also being published in India with culturally adapted case studies.

As a representative of the Evangelical Fellowship of Canada to the World Evangelical Alliance, Lynn connected with many International women. This has resulted in her being asked to speak and teach on the topics of gender, leadership and mentoring in various countries.

Lynn is married to the Rev. Roger Smith and they are both actively involved as layworkers in their local church community, Immanuel Baptist Church in Toronto which is affiliated with the Canadian Baptists of Ontario and Quebec.

As one of the founders of NextLEVEL Leadership in 2001, Lynn currently focuses on encouraging Christian women in the marketplace, profession or ministry to develop in the areas of character, competence and confidence in order to have a credible voice and be more effective in their leadership roles in the church and society.